SERMONS FOR SPECIAL SUNDAYS

by
Rev. Paul Pierpoint

Author of
Portraits of Truth: Sermons from Bible Characters

SCHMUL PUBLISHING COMPANY
NICHOLASVILLE, KENTUCKY

Copyright © 2018 by Schmul Publishing Co.
All rights reserved. No part of this publication may be reproduced or used in any form or by any means—graphic, electronic, or mechanical, including photocopying, recording, taping, or information storage or retrieval systems—without prior written permission of the publishers.

Churches and other noncommercial interests may reproduce portions of this book without prior written permission of the publisher, provided such quotations are not offered for sale—or other compensation in any form—whether alone or as part of another publication, and provided that the text does not exceed 500 words or five percent of the entire book, whichever is less, and does not include material quoted from another publisher. When reproducing text from this book, the following credit line must be included: "From *Sermons for Special Sundays* by Paul Pierpoint, © 2018 by Schmul Publishing Co., Nicholasville, Kentucky. Used by permission."

All biblical quotations are from the King James Bible unless otherwise noted.

Cover images copyrights: <a href='https://www.123rf.com/profile_compuinfoto'>compuinfoto / 123RF Stock Photo</a>; <a href='https://www.123rf.com/profile_vapi'>vapi / 123RF Stock Photo</a>; <a href='https://www.123rf.com/profile_anyka'>anyka / 123RF Stock Photo</a>. Used by permission.

Published by Schmul Publishing Co.
PO Box 776
Nicholasville, KY 40340
USA

Printed in the United States of America

ISBN 10: 0-88019-610-6
ISBN 13: 978-0-88019-610-9

Visit us on the Internet at www.wesleyanbooks.com, or order direct from the publisher by calling 800-772-6657, or by writing to the above address.

Contents

NEW YEAR'S SUNDAY
   1 GOALS FOR THE NEW YEAR 7
   2 OUR ASSURANCE OF ENCOURAGEMENT 19

PALM SUNDAY
   3 THE PARADE THAT WAS DIFFERENT 33

EASTER SUNDAY
   4 THE REALITY OF CHRIST'S RESURRECTION 43
   5 THE VICTORY OF EASTER 53

PENTECOST SUNDAY
   6 THE MEANING OF PENTECOST 67

MOTHER'S DAY
   7 QUALITIES OF AN EXEMPLARY MOTHER 83

FATHER'S DAY
   8 PRIORITIES OF A GOOD FATHER 91

INDEPENDENCE SUNDAY
    9   The Freedom Christ Brings 107

NATIONAL ADOPTION DAY
    10 Divine Adoption 119

THANKSGIVING
    11 The Grace of Gratitude 133

CHRISTMAS SUNDAY
    12 Wise Men Still Seek Christ 145
    13 Mary— Qualities to Follow 155
    14 The World's Greatest Gift 165

New Year's Sunday
Happy New Year!

1
GOALS FOR THE NEW YEAR
Psalm 4

As YOU STAND on the threshold of a new year, have you been thinking about the coming year? Have you thought about what changes you should or would like to make? Have you thought about setting some goals? Goal setting is a powerful tool for planning your future ministry. It can enable you to make vision a reality.

As you start your second cup of coffee, do some soul searching. What would you like to accomplish this coming year? The new year is a good time to stop and analyze your priorities, your values, and pursuits. It is a perfect time to evaluate your spiritual health and set goals for your growth.

Why set goals? In any realm if success is to be achieved, the establishment of goals is important. If this is true in the areas of education, business, and recreation, how much more important is the need for goals in the area of victorious Christian living? In seeking to live a life that pleases God, the establishment of goals can be very profitable. Growth in Christian living does not come automatically. Godly living is not aimless living.

In your meditation on the Psalms, look at psalm four. This is one of my favorite psalms. I see qualities that can serve as goals for godly living. This may not have been David's purpose in writing this psalm. However, in the process of setting goals for the new year, I found this psalm most helpful. What can we learn from it? What goals should we establish?

I. Make it your goal to *manage your problems.*

What about you? Do you have any problems? How do you cope with those problems, setbacks, and distresses that come to you in life? We all have our troubles. It seems some have even more than their share. Individuals today experience severe trials that are disrupting, discouraging. Such trials can be the loss of a job, a bitter divorce, terminal illness, financial reversals, death in the family, a fractured relationship, physical handicaps. Such problems can have a negative effect upon one's life emotionally, mentally, physically and spiritually. The question before us is, how do we respond?

In our meditation on this psalm, what can we learn from David? How did he handle his problems? It is evident the psalmist knew much about distress and adversity. There is not a biblical leader who had any more trouble. If anybody had reason to give up, David did.
- He was pursued by King Saul.
- He barely escaped several assassination attempts.
- He spent much time hiding in the wilderness.
- His friends turned against him. Some sought to kill him.
- Absalom his son led a revolt against his father.

Need I continue the list?

What did David do? First, let us note several things

David did not do. He did not put his problems on Facebook for all to see. "Look at all the troubles I am facing." He did not despair, throw in the towel, and become bitter. He did not say, "Where's God in all of this? Life does not make sense. Why did God do this to me?"

No, this was not David's response. Here is what he did do. David demonstrated a course of action which cannot be overlooked. When faced with adversity, David not only took his problems to the Lord, but he allowed God to use his adversities as tools for spiritual development. David allowed his problems to bring him closer to the Lord. He actually realized benefits from his troubles.

Listen to how David expresses it in Psalm 4:1, "…Thou hast enlarged me when I was in distress…." And in Psalm 119:71, "It is good for me that I have been afflicted; that I might learn thy statutes."

God may not deliver us from all our troubles. He may not deliver us from every trial. If we let Him, God would like to take some of our trials and transform them into tools for spiritual growth. Some of the best tools for shaping character in our lives are the tools of affliction. The hammering blows of hardship bring us closer to God. In my life and ministry, the most important lessons I have learned have come out of adversity. I have learned very little from prosperity. God knows what He is doing.

As you face this new year, make this one of your goals. Allow God to use your problems. He may have a divine purpose. Look for opportunities to turn your burdens into blessings. You may experience the fruit of adversity. Not all your trials may be ultimately ruinous. You do not have to become bitter—you can become better.

There is an interesting story from the life of Colonel Brengle, a former leader of the Salvation Army. One night as was his custom, he was ministering in a slum section in the city of London. He was witnessing for Christ in front of a saloon. Suddenly, a drunk man came by and flung a brick at Brengle. He fell against the doorway. His head became covered with blood. The blow could have killed him. Eventually, they took Brengle to the hospital. Long months of recovery ensued which prevented his involvement in any public ministry. Why would God allow this to happen?

During Brengle's eighteen months of convalescing, he began writing for the Salvation Army Journal. During this time, he wrote the valuable book, *Helps to Holiness*. This excellent book was translated into many languages. Over one-half million copies were printed. A number of people were brought to the Lord as a result of reading his book.

Much of this happened while he was still in the hospital. What was Brengle doing? Brengle was "managing" his problems. Yes, the trial was painful, but it became beneficial. No pain—no gain. No bricks—no books.

In our meditation on this psalm, what can we learn from David? Not only make it your goal to manage your problems...

II. Make it your goal to *master your priorities*.

As the new year approaches, you may want to think more about your priorities. What were your priorities last year? What changes should be made for the new year? What are the things you are living for? Is your focus solely on externals: fitness programs, financial plans, making money, career success, recreational and entertainment activities?

It is amazing how soon our priorities can become mixed up. It happens to the best of us. All of us are going at a run-away pace. The pressures of our modern culture can sometimes be overwhelming. Our lives can be so hectic. We must go here, go there. There are many things in life that are important. But we must discern what is most important.

Too many times we are majoring on the minors and minoring on the majors. Too many times our attention is consumed with lesser goals. There are those tasks we must do, and there are those activities we should do, and there are those things that are nice to do. Let us find out what we must do. There is a constant need to reexamine, to sort out, what is most important.

Start today. Review your priorities. Ask yourself these questions.
- What is the most important goal in my life?
- Is this goal being realized in my life?
- How do I spend my time?
- Am I managing my priorities properly?

As you look at this psalm, you cannot help but see David had some priorities.

In Christian living, we could mention a number of concerns that should be prioritized:
- the study of God's Word
- our time with the family
- keeping filled with the Spirit
- our concern for the lost

For this devotional, however, our focus is upon one priority found in this psalm. As we face the new year, make prayer a priority.

Let us think a little more about this priority. We cannot overlook the importance David gives to the subject of prayer. In this psalm and throughout the Psalms, we find David pouring out his heart to the Lord. In this psalm David demonstrates the priority of prayer.

Verse 1, "Hear me when I call, O God... have mercy upon me, and hear my prayer."

Verse 4, "...Commune with your own heart upon your bed, and be still."

Verse 5, "...Put your trust in the Lord."

Verse 6, "Lord, lift thou up the light of thy countenance upon us."

In the management of time, what place does prayer have? There is no area more important than prioritizing our time for prayer. For spiritual growth, for victorious living, for Christian service, you cannot overlook the priority of prayer.

What place does prayer have in my life? Do I need to make some adjustments? Look your prayer life over. It is not difficult for our prayer life to get crowded out. I confess I find this to be true in my life. Every once in a while I find my need to do some soul searching. Am I managing my priorities properly? Am I guarding my prayer time carefully?

Samuel Chadwick once said:

> The one concern of the devil is to keep Christians from praying. He fears nothing from prayerless work, prayerless religion. He laughs at our toil, mocks at our wisdom, but trembles when we pray. The best way to develop an abiding awareness of God's presence is to speak to Him often in prayer.

I remember well the last time R.G. Flexon preached from an Ohio convention platform. He was weak and feeble with age. But his message was far from weak. It was powerful. I share here the personal testimony he gave about being too busy in the work of the Lord.

> I was president of our college in the South. Not only was I president of a Bible school, I was also teaching six subjects a day. That load is enough for any one. I was also pastoring a nearby church in which I was preaching to about 150 people every Sunday. I was district superintendent of the Virginia District of Churches. I was keeping books for the school and running a small farm to help pay expenses. I was run-

ning a broom factory where thirty-six of our students were working to pay their way through school. I was doing some odd jobs on the side. I was working about eighteen hours a day trying to get the job done. One day I sat before my theological class of twenty-one young people. Most of them were young men preparing for the ministry. I had my Ralston's theology book open ready to teach, but I closed the book.

I told them, "Boys, something has happened to me. I've been preaching to you every Sunday. I have been teaching you theology, history and psychology during the week. But something has happened to me. The song birds have stopped making music in my heart, and I don't hear them anymore.

"Boys, I am not going to preach another sermon, I am not going to teach another class until the song birds start singing again. I am kneeling beside this chair, and I want you boys to gather around and put your hands on me and pray with me until God lets the song birds sing again."

We prayed for an hour. Something was happening in my soul. The song birds began to make a music, and I arose to my feet with the tears running down my checks, praising God. I said "Lord, if you help me, I don't want to get so busy again, even in the work of God, that the song birds stop making music in my soul."

Until the closing hours of his life, Rev. Flexon became known as a man who lived close to God, a man of prayer, a man whose ministry and missionary work became powerfully anointed of God. And we know the reason why. He took time to be with God.

This illustration may seem to be a little extreme, but we do need to be careful in guarding our prayer time. Do you have any prayer goals for your life this coming year?

I like the words of this old song:
> Have we trials and temptations?
> Is there trouble anywhere?
> We should never be discouraged;
> Take it to the Lord in prayer.
> Can we find a friend so faithful
> Who will all our sorrows share?
> Jesus knows our ev'ry weakness;
> Take it to the Lord in prayer.

In this psalm there is another priority suggested, another goal toward victorious living. Not only can you manage your problems and master your priorities...

III. Make it your goal to be *mindful of His presence.*

As we approach the new year, we might want to think about the importance of God's presence in our lives. Having His presence should be a top priority. It was so with David. In the psalm before us, there is a beautiful phrase in verse six: "Lord, lift thou up the light of thy countenance upon us." The word *countenance* gives us a pictorial representation of God's presence. What is so impressive, beyond this verse there is a constant reference involving his need of wanting God's presence. Psalm 51:11 says, "Cast me not away from thy presence; and take not thy holy spirit from me."

And that should be our concern. Really, this is more than a good new year's resolution. Having the presence of God in your life should be a lifelong passion, lifelong concern. But the fact is we can become careless, casual about this need. Keeping the presence of God is not something automatic.

One may ask, why is having His presence so important?

A. It brings the assurance of God's approval.

In your life there cannot be a higher goal, a greater desire, than to have the assuring presence of God manifested and magnified in your life. I like having the approval of others. But there is only one approval that matters. The most important in our life is God's approval. The controlling desire that sets a child of God apart from others is to sense the approving presence of God upon one's life.

Is this not what the psalmist was wanting? Verse six: "Lord, lift thou up the light of thy countenance upon us." Let the light of Thy face shine upon me. Let me know that I am yours. I want your approval. The psalmist talks much about the face of God which of course symbolizes His favor, His presence, His approval.

Why is having His presence so important?

B. It brings gladness of heart.

Our greatest joy comes from the abiding presence of the Lord. "Thou hast put gladness in my heart, more than in the time that their corn and their wine increased" (verse 7).

It is natural to desire happiness. But where is true happiness found? A good harvest brought joy to those people of Israel. But David tells us there is a joy one can have that has nothing to do with anything material. I do not deny the fact that this world has its "corn and wine," its kicks and thrills. But nothing can surpass the feeling of joy that comes from the presence of God dwelling in our hearts. The joy of the Lord is our strength.

It is interesting to see how many times David is found expressing his joy and praising God for His blessings. The book of Psalms itself is the praise book of the Bible. Listen to the psalmist: "Bless the Lord, O my soul: and all that is within me, bless his holy name" (Psalm 103:1).

The highest expression of our spiritual life is our praise to God. David teaches us that you can praise even through the dark shadows of life.

I will never forget the last time I heard my father testify. It was at Vermontville Camp. He started quoting the song, "Amazing grace, how sweet the sound." He never finished the song. The Holy Spirit came on Father with an uncontrollable joy. He started shouting, praising God. He wanted to run the aisles, but because of his infirmities, he could not. I will never forget, sitting near the front he asked his friend if he would run the aisles for him. His friend took off. The whole service became charged with the joyful presence of the Holy Spirit.

An occasion of cooperate praise like this will never be forgotten, But the fact is we do not have to be in a camp meeting to experience the joyful presence of God. As we begin this new year, would there be a need for more of His presence to shine upon our lives, bringing joy and gladness? The joy of the Lord is our strength. As with David, God is ready to put "gladness" in our hearts. Let's go for it.

> I have found the joy no tongue can tell.
> How it waves of glory roll!
> It is like a great o'erflowing well,
> Springing up within my soul.
> It is joy unspeakable and full of glory!

Why is having His presence so important?

C. It brings peace and security.

When experiencing His presence, we learn that happiness and peace go together. Psalm 4:8 says, "I will both lay me down in peace, and sleep: for thou, Lord, only makest me dwell in safety." It is a wonderful feeling to pillow your head at night and know that all your sins are forgiven, and if Jesus should come during the night, "Praise the Lord, I am ready!"

Friends, there is no pillow as soft as a good conscience. There is no bed as comfortable as the assurance of God's favor and presence. And someday, think of the peace of being ushered into God's very presence.

"Thou wilt keep him in perfect peace, whose mind is stayed on thee…" (Isaiah 26:3).

Have you finished your third cup of coffee yet?

We have been thinking about goals for the new year. I am of the firm conviction that God desires us to live in a way that fosters our spiritual development, increases our capacity to serve others, and instills a consistent sense of direction for the future. I also am convinced that a primary component of such living is the establishment and fulfillment of godly goals.

Usually you can easily discern whether or not a person has goals in his or her life. A person with clear cut, reasonable, and obtainable goals will demonstrate a sense of purpose in life. He will not be seen wandering aimlessly through life, going four steps in one direction, then three steps in another.

Perhaps you have heard of the story about the pilot who was lost. He said to his passengers, "I am not sure where we are going, but we are making good time." There are many people today making good time, but they lack defined direction. They do not know where they are going. Goal setting enables you to know where you are going. An individual with godly goals will know where he is headed and will have the persistence it will take to get there.

May I ask, what are your goals for this coming year? Is there a need to make some changes? We have offered three suggestions for your spiritual goal setting…

Make it your goal to manage your problems.

Make it your goal to master your priorities.

Make it your goal to be mindful of His presence.

A New Year, A New Beginning

The old year ends, a new begins
With pages clean and new;
And what is written on each page
Will now depend on you.

You can't relive the year that's past,
Erasing every wrong;
For once a year—or day—is spent,
It is forever gone.

But don't give up in dark despair
If you have failed some test;
Seek God's forgiveness and resolve
Henceforth to do your best.

Resolve each precious day to do
Things good and kind and pure;
Though days and years may pass away,
These things shall still endure.

You know not where your path may lead
Nor what's beyond the hill;
But know that God walks at your side,
If you will do His will.

All things are possible with God,
Though days be bright or dim;
So do your best and know that you
Can leave the rest to Him.

—Author Unknown

Have a blessed new year!

2
OUR ASSURANCE OF ENCOURAGEMENT
Psalm 46

As we face the new year, we have no knowledge of what will take place—good or bad. But there are some things we can do that will bring encouragement no matter what may take place.

Psalm 46 is not only one of my favorite psalms, but it is a good psalm to read as we move into the new year. Some key verses unlock for us timeless truths that need to be memorized. I enjoy seeing how David finds encouragement even in the worst of his trials

If I were to choose a title for this message, it would be this—Our Assurance of Encouragement.

I. First of all in this psalm, David describes for us his *need* for encouragement.

He gives us a graphic description of the turmoil he was facing in his day. I know the language here is symbolical, but look at these images: the mountains are trembling, the sea is raging. The very things he found security in are now falling apart—the earth is trembling. He was fearful. His dreams of supposed strength were being blasted. The psalmist needed a feeling of security, a feeling of encouragement.

Yes, times have changed. We live in a different world than that of the psalmist. But like the psalmist, we have our own need for encouragement, security and assurance. Needless to say, these are dark and difficult times—times fomenting with changes and challenges. You do not have to listen to Fox News to keep informed about the troublesome times in which we live.

Let us take a moment and list some of these causes for insecurity producing fear and uncertainty among our people, showing our need for assuring encouragement. We could preach a whole sermon from this point.

A. There is an insecurity that comes from *economic uncertainties*.

I am thinking about the financial problems of our country. Are we headed for another depression? Many have lost their jobs. Many companies have gone belly up. How much deeper can we go with our national debt? Yes, to say the least there is a fear that comes from an uncertain economy.

B. There is an insecurity that comes from the *threat of another terrorist attack*.

What tall towers are next to crumble? 9/11 tells us it can happen here in our country. It is unnerving. The question is not will it happen again, but when and where will it happen again?

C. There is an insecurity that comes from the *rise of natural disasters*.

There have never been so many earthquakes, tornados. floods, hurricanes as in the past few years.

D. There is an insecurity that comes from the *downward moral direction* of our country.

What is going to happen to our nation morally? Where will this moral drift take us? There is the problem of drugs, of illicit sex. I am thinking of so many homes being broken up. I am thinking of the youth of our day. They face temptation that we never faced twenty to thirty years ago. Youth today are surrounded with crazy options in the area of music, videos, games, dress, movies, pornography. There are those subtle temptations that come from modern technology—television, computers, cell phones, texting, drugs, drink. And on goes the list. To be honest about it, an earthquake has taken place in this area.

I have taken time to list some very disturbing situations. Now the question before us is this—what is our response to all this? Do we have to be overwhelmed by the troubles we face? Do we have to be ultimately discouraged or depressed? Does our faith have to be lost? Is there not some encouragement that we can experience? What can we learn from this psalm? How was it that David became encouraged, and how is it that we can become encouraged?

The psalmist speaks not only about the *need* of his assurance…

II. David describes for us the *nature* of encouragement.

No, he was not blind to the dangers about him, He was not ignorant of the perils of his day. He was not mindless of those "earthquakes" taking place. Where then did he find encouragement?

David lifts his eyes above his trials and troubles, and he shouts out (in words to this effect in verses 1, 2, 7, and 11), "God is our strength, a very present help in trouble. He is our security, our assurance of encouragement. The Lord of Hosts is with us. The God of Jacob is our refuge."

Alright! What is there about this God that brings security, removes needless fears, and brings encouragement? Our assurance of encouragement is based on four wonderful facts. First of all...

A. He is the God who is *existent*.

In our modern culture, there are some who question the reality of an eternal God. Put this down—the concept of an eternal God is not a myth. The first two words of the psalm are good enough to make me shout with joy. Did you read it? "God is! God is!"

I am an emotional being. I confess to you something happens to me when I read these words. It is like a tonic. My dear friends, GOD IS. No question about it. God is alive. God is real. He is not a myth. God is able to speak. God is able to communicate. God is all in all. God is our defender. God is our protector. God is our high tower. God is not dead—He is not even asleep. God is in control.

And what are the results of having this kind of God? We will not fear! He is a God who is existent. Friends, when things are cracking up all about us, when the mountains are skipping into the sea, we need to take a look at God. Our refuge is in God. And if our refuge is not in God, we have reason to fear—big time!

By the way the Bible never seeks to prove the existence of God. It just assumes it. If I did not believe in the existence of a holy powerful God, I would go bananas. I can understand why some commit suicide. There is no use, and there could be no use, But God is!

Many times I have heard Tony Anderson, the great evangelist of the Nazarene Church, say, "There are two things that God never had, and He will never have. One, He never had a cradle, and two, He never had a casket. If He had a cradle, I would like to know who was around to rock it? Who was around to sing its lullabies? And if He were to have a casket, who would be around to say the last farewell?"

Friends, what the psalmist is saying, and what I am simply saying, is this: the existence of God is the groundwork of our hope and confidence. It is our assurance of security! We do not have to fear!

> My hope is built on nothing less
> Than Jesus' blood and righteousness.
> I dare not trust the sweetest frame,
> But wholly lean on Jesus' name.
>
> His oath, His covenant, His blood
> Support me in the whelming flood.
> When all around my soul gives way,
> He then is all my Hope and Stay.

But our source, our assurance of encouragement is based on another fact. Not only is He the God who is existent...

B. He is the God who is *infinite*.

Verse one says, "God is our refuge and strength...." And there is no limit to His strength.

I love the revelation God gave to Abraham. Genesis 17:1, "And when Abram was ninety years old and nine, the Lord appeared to Abram, and said unto him, 'I am the Almighty God....'" In other words, "I am the infinite One." *Infinite One.* You can put your trust and confidence in Him. The All-Powerful One is our helper and strength in life.

- There is no limit to His strength — *infinite.*
- There is no measure to His power — *infinite.*
- There is no restriction to His knowledge — *infinite.*
- There is no shortage of His resources — *infinite.*
- He is no shriveled-up god.
- He is no puny being.

- He is the Sovereign of the Universe.
- He is not finite but *infinite*.
- He is not powerful, He is *all* powerful.
- He is not mighty, He is *almighty*.

I love the story found in Second Kings chapter six. We do not know why, but the king of Syria for some strange reason declared war on Israel. However, something went very wrong with his campaign. Every time he planned an attack or an ambush upon Israel, the king of Israel heard about it and prepared for it. This happened again and again. It happened so many times that the king of Syria was very sure he had a traitor in his camp.

One day he called one of his trusted officers and said very angrily, "Who in our army is for the king of Israel? Every time I plan an attack, the king of Israel knows about it."

Somebody came to the Syrian king and said, "No, my lord, you don't have a traitor. I will tell you what is happening, It's Elisha, the prophet that is in Israel. He tells the king of Israel what you plan for in secret. In fact it seems he knows what you are going to do before you even think it."

So the king of Syria says, "Well, that's easy. Let's go get Elisha, and our trouble will be over. Boys, Elisha is our target. Somebody go spy on him. Tell us where he is, and we will take care of him."

Someone says, "He lives in Dothan." What follows here is so amusing and amazing. Here this king orders the whole army into action—the artillery, the cavalry, the infantry. He gets this whole big group together and sends them down *en masse*, in great hosts. I have to laugh at all this. All this great military might to fight one man. What could old Elisha do against this great army? Well, I do not know what Elisha could do, but I do know what Elisha's God could do—and did do (verse 18).

Early next morning Elisha's servant looked out from the city wall and said, "Oh, my stars, I see Syrian horses and chariots all over the place." He was frightened. I am not sure, but I think Elisha was having his quiet time before the Lord when all of a sudden his servant breaks in excited. "Master, Master, we have had it. It is all over. The city of Dothan is encompassed about with enemy chariots and horses. They have surrounded the city. The enemy is upon us. Alas, Master, what are we going to do? Master, Master!"

What was Elisha's response? Elisha did three strange things. The first strange thing he did is found in his reply to his servant. Elisha said something strange to his servant— "Son, fear not!"

The servant replied, "Now wait a minute, Master. You say, 'Fear not.'" (By the way, that is the same word found in the forty-sixth psalm—we will not *fear*.)

Elisha was not troubled in the least. But the servant was. "Master, why do you say, 'Fear not?' We have troubles all over the place. I am out of a job. My mother in-law is coming to see me. The rent money is past due. My school bill is not paid. My boyfriend broke up with me. I have been so sick lately. A tornado is coming. The earth is quaking. The waters are troubled. And you tell me I should not be fearful. Master, are you not aware of the problems? You are not sick, are you?"

Elisha said something else that was strange. He said, "There is more with us than with them. We are on the winning side."

The servant could not believe what his master was saying. "Master, we don't even have an army. Nobody in Dothan is ready to fight. The only chariot we have has a flat tire. Do you have some sort of secret army?"

And in my sanctified imagination I can hear Elisha as he gets out his guitar and starts singing:

> There's more with us than be with them.
> We're on the winning side.
> With banners unfurled we'll tell the whole world
> That Jesus is captain and guide.
> There's nought to fear when He is near
> Though fierce the conflict may be.
> We'll never give in the fight against sin.
> With Christ there's victory.
>
> There's more with us than be with them.
> Lord, open our eyes to see
> The mountains around with chariots abound.
> We're trusting alone in Thee.
> The devil may boast and marshal his host
> And march in battle array.
> With Christ in the lead, we're sure to succeed.
> We're certain to win the day.

The third strange thing he did was he prayed. Well, what is so strange about praying? Well, it was not strange *that* he prayed; it was *how* he prayed. How did he pray? He did not pray, "Lord, destroy that wicked army. Send fire from heaven." No, no. How did he pray? "Lord, open this young man's eyes that he may see."

"Master, Master, don't pray that way. My eyes are already open." But really his eyes were not open. They were closed. They were closed to the reality of God's *infinite power.*

And that is precisely the trouble with us. We need to get our eyes open. Our eyes of faith need to be opened. We need to see that God is bigger than our difficulties. We need to see that God is bigger than the devil. "If God be for us, who can be against us (Romans 8:31)?" We need to see when everything in life is being removed, when all the powers of hell are let loose against us. We need to see that God is still in control. He is still on the throne.

By the way God answered that prophet's prayer. That young man's eyes became open. And when he got his eyes opened, the scene changed immediately. The servant cried, "Look at them. Look at them." For every horse, for every chariot, for every soldier, he saw a host of angelic powers. Behold, the mountain was filled with them. The Lord of Hosts is with us!

With one stroke the whole army was struck with blindness, and Elisha met the leaders of the Syrian army milling about in their blindness. God took care of the problem.

"The Lord of hosts is with us. The God of Jacob is our refuge" (Psalm 46:7).

But our source, our assurance of encouragement is based on another fact. Not only is He the God who is *existent*, not only is He is the God who is *infinite*,

C. He is the God Who is *present*.

Verse 1— "God is our refuge and strength, a very present help in trouble." Let me give you a paraphrase of this verse. "God is our refuge, one who is very near at hand, One who is ever present in the nick of time."

Years ago, the Pierpoints lived in North Troy, New York. Father was a pastor of a church in that small city. Back in those days we did not belong to the affluent set. In fact it was not too far removed from the depression era. Most holiness preachers in those days could say with Peter and John, "Silver and gold have I none." I think of the toys our children have today. All of this would be unheard of back in the '30s. I did not have a bicycle until I started working as a paperboy for the Morning Sun route. I was well into my teens then.

I love to ride a bike, As a young kid I dreamed of owning a bike someday. I guess that is why when Daddy would say to the family, "Let's go and see our folks in Binghamton," my heart would leap for joy. I would get to see my cousin Wilbur. Or should I say, I would get to see my cousin Wilbur's bike. I would get to ride his bike. Wow! I did not care much for Wilbur, but I cared for his bike.

I will never forget those trips to Binghamton. It seemed like we would never get there. That would be the old Route 7 from Schenectady to Binghamton. But we would finally make it. What a joy to see the city and finally turn into the last street. We would turn off Chenango Street and take the street where my relatives lived. And guess what? Right there out in plain sight by my cousin's porch was Wilbur's bike. Why I did it, I do not know. I never asked my father. I did not take the time to look for Wilbur. But I ran to his bike and took off. I guess I had a lot of pent up energy from that long ride.

I did not know the streets in those days. Years later I pastored in the city of Binghamton. But I took off down Bevier Street and to the corner of State Street. And there on that corner, I met the town bully. I suppose every town has one. This bully was a monster, a big ugly old fellow. He saw me, ran after me, caught me, and knocked me off Wilbur's bike.

Man, I have heard of stealing bikes in the dark. This guy was after the bike in broad daylight with me riding on it, and I was scared. I grabbed hold of the bike and tried to tell him that he could not have it, but it made no difference with him. He hit me again as he was determined to take that bike. He hit me again and knocked me for a loop, but again I grabbed hold of the bike.

We were in a battle. The old monster was beating on me, but I was determined to hold out to the end. But I could see the end coming. Just when I was about to lose her, all of a sudden my daddy came down the street by that corner in his '40 Ford. He stopped at the intersection. He was about to pull out when he saw his only boy in mortal combat. Daddy quickly surveyed the situation. He saw his boy in deep trouble.

Daddy screeched those brakes and lunged out that door. And that old bully took off. My father met my need. Had he come earlier, I would not have needed him—no danger. Had he come later, it would have been all over for me. But he came just in the nick of time. My despair turned to delight. My defeat changed into victory. Assurance replaced insecurity. It had nothing to do with me and everything to do with my father. He was an ever present help in time of trouble.

And, friends, that is just like our Heavenly Father. I do not know who your town bully is, but know that your God is bigger than the town bully. And more than that, He is a present help in time of need—ready. Your despair turned to delight, your defeat changed into victory. Friends, God knows who you are. He knows where you are. He knows about the town bully. He knows how much you can take. He knows how much grace you need. He is bigger than the town bully.

Palm Sunday

3
THE PARADE THAT WAS DIFFERENT
Luke 19:28-44

I DO NOT KNOW anyone who does not like a parade. We often have parades to celebrate certain events. In our little town of Hobe Sound we have a Christmas parade. Many of us would not miss that annual event. Several years ago, our Hobe Sound Academy Band won first prize in the parade.

Then there are the large national parades: Macy's Thanksgiving Day Parade in New York City, St. Patrick's Day parades, July 4th parades, and many others.

Sometimes we have parades to honor certain individuals such as astronauts, senators, and military heroes. In these parades we find distinguished leaders marching, flags waving and decorated floats leading. Much preparation is involved to make these parades a success.

For this study I want to share with you a story about another parade. It is a story that goes back 2,000 years. It is a story of a different kind of parade. In this parade there were no academy bands playing. There were no gun salutes. Instead of flags or banners waving, the crowds were waving palm branches and shouting, "Hosanna to the King." What is the story involving this parade? Palm Sunday is a good time to talk about this interesting event.

Thousands of pilgrims were streaming into the city to attend the large Passover feast in Jerusalem. On their way it was being told that this popular miracle worker from Nazareth was also on His way to Jerusalem. Excitement was mounting. By this time Jesus was becoming known all across the country. It was being told how people were healed, the lame could walk, the blind could see. In fact just before His march into Jerusalem, Jesus brought a dead man back to life.

Learning of His coming, great crowds left Jerusalem to greet this miracle worker. The road was lined with people throwing their coats and palm branches in front of Jesus to celebrate the arrival of their King. They shouted, "'Hosanna: Blessed is the King of Israel that cometh in the name of the Lord.' (John 12:13) Hail to the King of Israel!"

This was the beginning action of a parade never to be forgotten. While there have been many parades displaying great pomp and pageantry, this has to be the greatest. I would love to have been there on that triumphal entry. There must have been a lot of excitement.

On this Sunday one week before Easter, Christians will be remembering Jesus' short trip from Bethany to Jerusalem. What was there about this parade that made it so different? Are there lessons we can learn from this event?

I. It was a parade led by a young, untried donkey.

As Jesus started His procession into Jerusalem, He stopped and surprised His disciples. Jesus asked His disciples to do a very strange thing. "Boys, go in town. Standing by a gate, you will find a young donkey whereon never man sat. I want you to untie that donkey and bring it to me. If the owner says anything, you are to say, 'The Lord needs him.'" (Luke 19: 28-31)

I am sure the disciples wondered about this request, "What is His need of a donkey? He has never done this before. As a king, should not He enter in a chariot or riding on a prancing stallion? But come to Jerusalem riding a young colt that has never been ridden—that's strange."

But the disciples were obedient. They did exactly as they were told. Is there not a lesson here for us? What God wants for our lives may seem strange. But we must remember, God knows what He is doing. A Sovereign God knows what is best. We can trust His guidance.

All the way my Savior leads me.
What have I to ask beside?
Can I doubt His tender mercy
Who through life has been my Guide?
—Fanny Crosby

II. It was a parade with a prophetic promise.

This parade was unique in that it was predicted in prophecy. Five hundred years before the birth of Christ, the prophet Zechariah wrote about the coming Messiah. He told the Jewish people they would recognize their king by His triumphal entry into Jerusalem. (Zechariah 9:9)

On Palm Sunday Jesus fulfilled this prophecy. "The Lord is not slack concerning His promise" (II Peter 3:9). The Palm Sunday parade was just one more proof that Jesus keeps His promises.

It is interesting to study those Scriptures dealing with prophecy. This is one of those important prophecies which was fulfilled in Christ's earthly life.

III. It was a parade divided by conflict.

How was this parade different? The shouting voices were not all voices of praise. Not everybody was happy. Unlike modern parades today, this was a parade that was divided. While the crowds were praising Jesus, there were those criticizing Jesus. The Sadducees and Pharisees were among those who were deeply disturbed. By no means were they waving any palm branches of praise. The religious leaders even tried to get Jesus to silence the crowd. But Jesus responded that even if they were silent, the stones would cry out in praise.

Why were those religious leaders furious seeing the people praising Jesus? There was a deep fear that they would lose their power and influence over the people. After all, the Pharisees were the spiritual leaders, the keepers of the law. And give them credit—these Pharisees sought to preserve the laws given by Moses. For this they could not be faulted. The problem, however, was they added many commandments of their own making. These commandments became as important as the laws of Moses. They must be kept. They gave equal authority to oral traditions and rules differing from God's law. And the contention was, you are not living right unless you keep all these rules.

Yes, obeying God's laws is important. Having standards for Christian living is necessary. We need to guard our attitudes and actions. But we are never saved by following some rules. No matter how good a life we live, we cannot be saved apart from God's saving grace.

Perhaps for the Pharisees jealousy played a role in their opposition to the Master. They were being overlooked. Their control was being threatened. Here is a crowd flocking to see Jesus, not the Pharisees. The crowd was praising Jesus, not the Pharisees. This was not to be. With these so-called keepers of the law, we see displayed the ugliness of envy and jealousy.

What can we learn from this? At times even religious people are not free from developing some form of envy. Jealousy can be so divisive, destructive. Jealousy is often the root of many bad relationships and divisions in the church. We should guard against a spirit of envy.

IV. It was a parade involving a crying leader.

Parades are often happy occasions. Normally, this would have been a happy event. There was a lot of joy, shouting, cheering, and waving. But there was sorrow involved. You do not generally cry in parades. Yet this parade was different. They call this parade the *Triumphal Entry*, but actually we should call it the *Tearful Entry*.

What happened? To the crowd's surprise, the procession stopped. I am sure those who were ahead wondered what happened. They hurried back to see what had gone wrong. They soon found out. They found Jesus crying. The King was weeping, and they were real tears. "And when he was come near, he beheld the city, and wept over it" (Luke 19:41).

Why was He weeping? These were not tears of self-pity. These were not tears of some personal discontent. I am sure He is thinking about the pain that will come with those piercing rusty nails which would suspend Him on a cruel cross. But He is not weeping for Himself.

Why was He weeping?

A. He saw the persistence of their rejection. "...How often would I have gathered thy children together, ...and ye would not" (Matthew 23:37). I sometimes think this phrase is the saddest and darkest phrase in the Bible: *ye would not*.

1. Here is the voice of an aching heart.
2. Here is infinite compassion.

3. Here are outstretched arms. "Jerusalem, Jerusalem, I would gather you in. But ye would not." Jesus stopped the parade and wept.

B. Why did Jesus weep when He saw Jerusalem? Having the omniscience of God, Jesus knew these fickle people who were crying out, "Hosanna!" would soon be shouting, "Crucify Him!"
1. He knew Judas, one of His handpicked disciples, would betray Him.
2. He knew another disciple, Peter, would deny Him.
3. He knew Caiaphas the high priest would conspire with Pilate the Roman governor to bring about His death.
4. And He knew the future of Jerusalem. Looking ahead forty years, He saw the destruction that would come upon the city at the hands of the Emperor Titus and his Roman legions.

C. Jesus also wept because His ministry was almost over. Time was short. He had healed their sick; He had raised their dead; He had cleansed their lepers, fed their hungry. And John 1:11 says, "He came unto his own, and his own received him not." And so He wept. This broke His heart, and it still does. Unbelief and rejection breaks God's heart because He knows the consequences.

V. It was a parade with great enthusiasm.

You talk about a crowd. In this parade some were reacting critically to the cheering, excited audience. Their voices of criticism, however, were drowned out by the awesome shouts of praise. The shouts of "hosanna" were heard all over the place. And it is not hard to think of the reasons for their praise. Some hailed Him with joy, welcoming Him as an earthly king come to establish the throne of David.

A. Among the crowd would be people He had healed. Perhaps Bartimaeus was there, a man who had received his sight. How about those lepers who had been rejoicing for the healing they received?

B. Many had seen His miracles—the lame could walk, the deaf could hear, demons were cast out.

C. And on goes the list, all praising Him for the mighty works they had seen. (Luke 19:37) They were anxious to see this miracle worker.

On this Palm Sunday as we approach Easter, I wonder if we could spend a little extra time praising the Lord. Let us reflect on all He has done for us. Let us pause and give Him thanks. We do not have to wave branches in a parade to do this. I am reminded of the words of the hymn written by Ernest Shurtleff:

Lead on, O King Eternal,
The day of march has come;
Henceforth in fields of conquest
Thy tents shall be our home.
Through days of preparation
Thy grace has made us strong,
And now, O King Eternal,
We lift our battle song.

Lead on, O King Eternal,
We follow, not with fears;
For gladness breaks like morning
Where'er Thy face appears;
Thy cross is lifted o'er us;
We journey in its light:
The crown awaits the conquest;
Lead on, O God of might.

Easter Sunday

4
THE REALITY OF CHRIST'S RESURRECTION
I Corinthians 15:12-20

I INVITE YOU TO turn to I Corinthians 15. It is the greatest chapter found anywhere in the Bible on the subject of the resurrection. True Christianity is the religion of the resurrection. It is the keystone of the Christian faith. Because of the importance of this fact, no truth has been under so much attack as the resurrection of Jesus Christ. It was a reality in Paul's day. It is so in our day.

It is not surprising to think there should be opposition to this truth outside the church. When the Apostle Paul was preaching the resurrection in Athens, the center of Greek culture, they laughed at him. Then the Jewish society had their sad sector that did not believe in the resurrection at all.

What was even more astounding, the apostle was facing some opposition within the church. There were people in Corinth who did not believe in the doctrine of the resurrection. There were those who did believe in Christ's resurrection exclusively. They said, "Dead men don't rise again." Paul said, "…How say some among you that there is no resurrection of the dead" (verse 12)?

And thus, under the inspiration of the Holy Spirit, Paul takes his quill in hand and with forceful logic sets about to refute the arguments of his skeptics. And he does it in a magnificent manner.

Easter is a reality. It is not a myth. On Easter we celebrate the most glorious and important event in the history of the world.

From this passage let us focus our attention on verses twelve to twenty. There are three considerations concerning the reality of His resurrection.

I. There is an *assumption* that is dreadful.

First Corinthians 15:14 begins with this interesting phrase. It is an unthinkable phrase, "And if Christ be not risen…." What a terribly oppressive assumption this is! There are many times in life when *if* might have made all the difference in the world.

- If the captain of the Titanic would have listened to the warnings given him, hundreds of lives would have been saved.
- If they had caught those wicked hijackers who sent those planes into the twin towers, three thousand lives would have been saved.
- If my preacher friend had only gone to the doctor sooner, he probably would be alive today.

And we could go on with the list. You could make your own personal lists of "what if" statements. However, the most oppressive, unthinkable *if* is found in our text. What *if* Christ is not risen from the dead? What *if* Easter is not true?

As we look at this passage, I want you to observe some of the oppressive conclusions that come from this dreadful assumption. Obviously, the apostle is using reverse logic here to actually show the importance of Christ's resurrection. Paul states a number of tragic things that will happen if Easter is not true.

A. Our *preaching* is profitless.

Verse 14: "And if Christ be not risen, then is our preaching vain..." The word *then* is an important one. I want you to feel the ironic force of this statement—then what happens? Then the unthinkable happens. Without an Easter our preaching is an empty voice—vain, no reality. It may be full of sound and fury, but it signifies nothing. No substance. The word *vain* means: empty, futile, with no purpose, a colossal waste of time.

If there were no Easter, forget the teaching and preaching of the Apostle Paul. The apostle lived a wasted life. He wrapped himself up in a cause that meant nothing—*profitless*. But let us not stop with Paul and the other early apostles. Through the centuries of Christianity, our world has known other great preachers who proclaimed the risen Christ. Were their voices just empty noise—spreading meaningless nonsense—perpetuating a lie?

Through the lens of history we can view the founder of Methodism, John Wesley, standing in village squares preaching to a crowd of common people. Often times his crowd was made up of miners, tears streaming down black-covered faces. Wesley spent his entire life traveling by horseback preaching to thousands of people. One time he even climbed on his father's tomb using it for a pulpit. That was something for this dignified Anglican preacher to do. *If* Christ be not risen, his preaching was nothing more that empty prattle. Wesley was spending his life spreading nonsense.

What else can we say of the preaching of Whitfield and Asbury, Finney and Moody, and a host of others? Without the reality of Easter, it was empty noise. Today we likewise have no good news to share if our founder is still in the tomb. We are liars. Christ's resurrection brings credibility to our preaching.

In verse fourteen he mentions something else. If Easter is not true, not only is preaching profitless…

B. Our *faith* is groundless.

If there is no resurrection of the dead, then "…your *faith* is also vain" (verse 14). It is void of reality. It has no foundation. There is nothing for faith to lay hold of. There is no ground to stand on. There is no foundation. Who wants to put his faith in Jesus if He is dead and not who He claimed to be?

This is the difference between Jesus Christ and the founders of other religions. Other leaders lived, they died, and are still in the grave. But Jesus lived, He died, and He rose again! Friend, there is no need to follow a loser.

The Bible tells us in the book of Romans, "(He is) declared to be the Son of God with power…by the resurrection from the dead" (Romans 1:4). The resurrection from the dead is God's stamp of approval. We do not serve a dead Christ—a dead Savior is nobody's Savior. Everything in our Christian religion stands or falls on the literal resurrection of Jesus Christ from the grave!

A little boy was in the classroom, and the teacher gave this assignment: write an essay on the world's greatest living man. Some wrote about the president, some about members of congress. Some wrote about people in the entertainment world. Others wrote about sports figures, scientists and philosophers. But one little boy wrote about Jesus Christ. When the teacher received the paper, she said, "Son, that's a nice paper, but you misunderstood the assignment. I said the world's greatest 'living' man." He said, "But, teacher, He *is* alive!"

He is *alive*! We do not serve a dead Savior. Thank you, John, for your testimony: *He is alive!*

In verse fifteen, the apostle mentions a third dreadful

assumption. Not only is *preaching* profitless and our *faith* groundless...

C. Our *witness* is worthless.

Verse fifteen: "Yea, and we are found false witnesses of God..." Do you know what a false witness is? That is somebody who testifies in a courtroom and knowingly, willingly, deliberately lies. His statements are not true. He is not telling the truth.

The twelve disciples were eyewitnesses to the risen Christ. Were they false witnesses? This assumption would make them liars. Were they hallucinating when they thought they saw Him and even touched Him? Was this some sort of dream? How can we be sure they did not just make up a story about Jesus to save face?

This was not a made-up story as most of these disciples paid with their very life's blood for their testimony and faith in Jesus Christ. They suffered, they bled, they died because they believed in Jesus Christ. If they were liars, they had to endure a lot for a falsehood.

Hypocrites and martyrs are not made of the same stuff. A man may live for a lie, but few will die for it. Nobody dies willingly for what he knows to be a lie. These people did not die trusting in a delusion. We know tradition tells us that Peter was put on a cross. The disciples were no con artists. Do not tell me that Paul was a liar or that Peter was a rascal or that John was faking it. I do not believe it, Again, people do not generally die for a lie. All the disciples declared repeatedly that Christ had risen. There would be no Easter if Christ is still in that grave.

Here is another dreadful effect. Not only is *preaching* profitless, our *faith* groundless, and our *witness* worthless—are you ready?

Without an Easter...

D. Our *future* would be hopeless.

Is our hope of eternal life just a dream? Friends, you take the resurrection out of Christianity, you have no hope. No light would ever beak across our sky.

Our enemy would never be destroyed. Paul is talking about the enemy of death. (verse 26) What a horrible thing to think that this monster *death* will never come to an end. (verse 32) The monster death would have reigned supreme. There is no future for us. Our dreams would never be realized. (verse 49) Forget the prospect of heaven. If Christ is still in the grave, He will not be in heaven to prepare a place for you. The splendors of that heavenly world will never be realized.

Again, if there is no Easter…

E. Our *salvation* is meaningless.

First Corinthians 15:17: "And if Christ be not raised, your faith is vain; ye are yet in your sins." What does this mean? If Christ is still in the grave, sin is sovereign. There is no salvation. It would be a salvation only in name. Without the reality of Easter, we would be lost sinners forever.

Why is this? What is the reason for this? The *atonement* for sin would not have been completed. In our salvation you cannot separate the cross from the resurrection. They belong together. In thinking about our redemption, there is a tendency to make the cross exclusive. It was my sins that put Him to the cross. But if my sins had kept Him there, I would have been dammed forever.

The saving effects of the atonement would not have been perfected without the resurrection. His resurrection not only vindicates His claims, it validates our forgiveness. He was delivered for our offences and was raised for our justification. (Romans 4:25) Christ's resurrection is necessary for our justification. And with the full payment made, we can sing,

Jesus paid it all;
All to Him I owe.
Sin had left a crimson stain;
He washed it white as snow.

We have spent enough time looking at this long train of dismal consequences if we only had a dead Christ. Look now at the change of feeling in I Corinthians 15:20. We move from fiction to fact! We move from despair to hope and from death to life, grief to gladness. The nightmare of dark assumptions is over. "But now is Christ risen!"

Thank God for our proof of His resurrection. Thank God for the reality of Easter.

In this chapter we find an *assumption* that is dreadful, but the apostle does not stop there. Thank God, there is another truth spoken of.

II. There is an *affirmation* that is factual.

Thank God for the proof of His resurrection. There are several facts involved affirming the reality of His resurrection. These irrefutable facts remove all doubt.

Fact #1: There is the testimony of the *Scriptures*.

In chapter fifteen verse three, the apostle stated that his teaching was no invention of his own. This was not his opinion or viewpoint. This was not something he conjured up. But according to the Scriptures, Christ died for our sins, He was buried, and He rose again on the third day. Even the Old Testament predicted Christ's death, burial and resurrection. You are in serious trouble if you cannot accept the validity of the Scriptures.

Fact # 2: There is the testimony of *eyewitnesses*.

Jesus was seen alive by many different people. The list is long: Mary Magdalene, the two Marys together, Simon

Peter, the two believers on the road to Emmaus. He also appeared to the disciples in the upper room. I Corinthians 15:6 "…He was seen of above five hundred brethren at once…" Could all these people have been deceived?

Fact #3: There is the testimony of *special witnesses*.

Verse 8: "And last of all he was seen of me also, as of one born out of due time." Paul was not among the original apostles. But he saw Jesus with his own eyes. And he tells us what happened. With testimonies of this nature, am I going to believe that Jesus is still in the grave? Am I going to believe that all there is to life is just this earthly existence? There is no future life? No, friend, I cannot believe that. I cannot accept that.

Fact #4: There is the testimony of *changed lives*.

The fact is the believers who saw the risen Christ were drastically changed. They were convinced of Jesus' resurrection. A total change came over them They went with boldness preaching the living Christ. Why? Because they knew He was alive! As far as I am concerned, this is one of the most thrilling testimonies proving the certainty of Christ's resurrection. The changes that took place could not be accounted for any other way. Proofs of the resurrection are overwhelming.

In talking about the reality of His resurrection, we come to our last point. In this chapter we find there is not only an *assumption* that is dreadful, and an *affirmation* that is factual…

III. There is an *anticipation* that is delightful.

In this chapter the apostle lists for us some delightful things we can expect. It is a joy to look over this list. What are some of these benefits that can be anticipated?

A. Our *labors* will be rewarded.

The Scriptures intimate to us that the Lord takes note of our labors and will reward them. "Therefore, my beloved brethren... your labor is not in vain in the Lord" (verse 58).

It is nice to have our friends praise us for our work. But there is nothing more rewarding than to have the Master's blessing on our labors. If we are faithful and careful in our labors, think of the reward that awaits us in heaven.

B. Our *bodies* will be resurrected.

Verse 52 says, "In a moment, in the twinkling of an eye, at the last trump: for the trumpet shall sound, and the dead shall be raised incorruptible, and we shall be changed."

What kind of body will this be? (verses 42-43) It will be an incorruptible body. It will be a body raised in glory—raised in power. There will be a newness of life—no more sickness, suffering, no more death. It will be a spiritual body, a resurrected body. Fascinating!

C. Our *dreams* will be realized.

There is a place in God's tomorrow that He has prepared for us that beggars all descriptions. We cannot imagine what it is going to be like. It is a part of our dreams. What will heaven be like? Just the city of Jerusalem will be fascinating. It is a city that will have gold for its streets—pearls for its gates—jasper for its walls. There will be no hospitals there—no cancer patients—no sickness of any kind. There will be no police roaming the streets of Jerusalem. There will be no funeral homes in heaven. All sorrow will be wiped away. That is just in the city of Jerusalem.

But hold on! The great thrill of our lives is more than seeing a place—it is seeing a person! My anticipation of seeing Christ will be thrillingly realized. And someday

soon, He is coming for His people. *Oh, glorious day!*
> Above the waves of earthly strife,
> Above the ills and cares of life,
> Where all is peaceful, bright and fair,
> My home is there, my home is there.

5
THE VICTORY OF EASTER
Romans 1:1-7

For many people, Easter is nothing more than a spring break on the beaches of Daytona or Fort Lauderdale or night clubbing in Palm Springs. For others it is family reunion time or an Easter egg hunt. Traditionally, Easter is also a time for wearing bright new clothes to welcome the sunshine of spring after a long cold winter.

Let us pause in our celebrations of spring and remember the true meaning of Easter. It is more than a break from college or shopping for a new outfit. Easter should be a time set aside for worship. Easter involves the celebration of the greatest event this world has ever known.

A few years ago, a unique survey was conducted. Twenty-eight educators and historians were asked to examine all the major events that have ever happened in the world. Their assignment was to report on what they considered to be the one hundred most significant events to occur in the history of mankind. In the history of the world, only one hundred events could be selected.

After several months the panel reconvened. Much research and deliberation had taken place. The group reported on what they considered to be the most significant events in the history of the world. A couple of those monumental events included the discovery of America and the invention of the printing press—and the list goes on. What is so sad is the person and life of Jesus appears last on the list. Disturbing indeed. In the life of Christ alone, you are seeing the world's most influential person. His life was one of miraculous events—healing, raising the dead, serving others. It was a life of triumphant spiritual victories. No earthly life was ever lived like the life of our Master.

There was one life which altered the course of human history. What were the educators and historians thinking?

In the life of Christ on earth, there is an occurrence which cannot be overlooked. This was the most revolutionary event to occur in human history. It was the victory of Easter—the glorious resurrection of Christ!

For our encouragement and instruction in this Easter message, I would like to list for you some of the practical outworkings of the victory of Easter—the benefits of Easter. My heart is full of praise when I think of all that was accomplished on that Easter occasion. No, we are not celebrating just a great life. We are celebrating a great victory.

In the victory of Easter…

I. We see the outworking of divine power.

Along with many other of his verses, I like what the Apostle Paul had to say about Christ's Resurrection. He saw *power* as being one of the descriptive benefits of Easter. Christ is "declared to be the Son of God with power…by the resurrection from the dead" (Romans

1:4). Later in his Philippian letter he testifies, "That I may know him, and the power of his resurrection..." (Philippians 3:10).

What was this power? Go back to that day of infamy — those dark hours of Calvary.

It is an historical fact, Jesus died on the Cross.

His side was pierced through.

Jesus' friends removed His lifeless body from the cross.

He was buried in a borrowed tomb.

His body was wrapped in linen cloth.

The grave was guarded by a legion of Roman soldiers. It was sealed by a Roman seal.

To the followers of Jesus, the end of the world had come.

Peter was headed back to his nets brokenhearted.

Mary sobbed with grief.

Cleopas, struggling with mistaken expectations, would soon begin a dreary walk back to Emmaus.

It was all over. Their dreams were dashed.

The light of the world seemed to be extinguished.

Then something glorious happened. On that third morning the lifting, liberating power of His resurrection was released. HE AROSE!

Death could not hold Him.

Darkness could not hinder Him.

The Roman soldiers could not stop Him.

The great stone could not block Him.

The Roman seal could not contain Him.

Bodily decay could not destroy Him.

He walked out of that tomb the mighty conquering Christ, victorious over death and the grave! No greater power has ever been displayed in the history of this world than what happened in those early Easter hours. Expressing the greatness of that Easter morning, Robert Lowry wrote one of my favorite Easter hymns.

Up from the grave He arose,
With a mighty triumph o'er His foes;
He arose a victor from the dark domain,
And He lives forever with His saints to reign.
He arose! He arose!
Hallelujah! Christ arose!

In the victory of Easter...

II. We see deliverance over the slavery of sin.

Romans 6:6 "Knowing this, that our old man is crucified with him, that the body of sin might be destroyed, that henceforth we should not serve sin."

Romans 4:25 "Who was delivered for our offences, and was raised again for our justification."

From the very beginning of time, man has faced the serious problem of sin. Because we are descendants of Adam, we have inherited from him a depraved nature—a sinful nature. The apostle freely speaks about this condition.

Romans 5:12 "Wherefore, as by one man sin entered into the world, and death by sin; and so death passed upon all men, for that all have sinned."

Romans 7:24 "O wretched man that I am! who shall deliver me from the body of this death?"

The question remains, can one be delivered from this problem of sin? Is salvation possible? With a heart full of praise we can shout out the answer—Yes! His resurrection made redemption possible! He "was delivered for our offences, and was raised again for our justification" (Romans 4:25). The serious problem of sin was dealt with in the victory of Easter. Those who put their trust in Christ can have victory over Satan and enjoy freedom from the bondage of sin. "I thank God through Jesus Christ our Lord" (Romans 7:25).

Over the years during my pastoral ministry, I have seen a number of individuals powerfully delivered from the enslavement of sin. I am thinking now of a very close friend of mine who faithfully served churches for years in the state of New York. You would never believe the kind of life he lived as a young man. Warren was bound by the chains of sin. He was addicted to alcohol, at times coming home drunk. His wife was a chain smoker. Their marriage was in trouble—divorce seemed inevitable.

But I will never forget what happened. Providentially, Christian neighbors developed a very helpful and close relationship. On one occasion they succeeded in getting Warren and his wife to go with them to a revival service in a nearby church. The evangelist, under the anointing of the Spirit, preached that God can wonderfully change your life. He talked about the importance of salvation and gave a clear gospel call. At the end of the message the evangelist gave an invitation to receive Christ.

During the invitation, Warren's wife said, "Honey, that's what we need. Both of us need to make some changes." Somewhat reluctantly Warren followed his wife to an altar of prayer. That event became a turning point in their lives. They saw their need for a deliverance from the habits of sin and experienced transformation. They found joy as they began serving the Lord with newfound freedom in Christ.

Even Warren was willing to make some changes. In time the drink habit was gone, the substance abuse was disbanded, their marriage was strengthened. This couple became a wonderful example of the liberating power of the gospel.

Warren and his family chose to make our church their home church. As their pastor and close friend, what a thrill it was to see their warm acceptance of our church's ministry and the evidenced desire of becoming what God wanted them to be.

Several years later, Warren came to my office and poured out his heart: "Pastor, I need your guidance. I feel like God is calling me to preach." After some study and preparation, Warren entered the ministry and became a holiness preacher and pastor of one of the largest churches in the area.

Thank God, there is deliverance from the bondage of sin. A life can be wonderfully changed. This is the story of Warren.

In the victory of Easter...

III. We see divine promises fulfilled.

In discussing the benefits of Easter, there are promises Jesus gave to His disciples. During His life on earth, Jesus did a very daring thing. On five occasions he predicted that though He would be killed in Jerusalem, He would rise the third day. Only a fool would say he is going to rise three days after he dies. But our Master was not a fool. His promises were fulfilled.

In Jesus' teaching there is everywhere this note of anticipated victory. When Jesus spoke of His approaching death, He always associated with it the truth of resurrection. Listen to the Master as He speaks: "Destroy this temple, and in three days I will raise it up" (John 2:19). "...The Son of man must suffer many things, ...and be killed, and after three days rise again" (Mark 8:31). On the Mount of Transfiguration He talked about His soon departure which He was about to bring to fulfillment at Jerusalem. (Luke 9:31)

As we read these Gospel accounts, it's thrilling to see the fulfilling of these promises. They all took place at Easter.

You remember the story of Mary Magdalene? She came to the tomb looking for the Master's dead body. What a surprise! The angel of the Lord met her at the entrance and said to her, "...Do not be alarmed and frightened, for I know that you are looking for Jesus, Who was crucified. He is not here; He has risen, as He said [He would do]...." (Matthew 28:5-6 AMPC). This must have been an exciting time as Christ's promise to her was being fulfilled.

In talking about divine promises, I am thinking now of those promises the Lord has given to us in His Word. These are promises for our day!

Let us look at some of them.

Matthew 5:8— "Blessed are the pure in heart: for they shall see God."

Matthew 6:6— "But when you pray, go into your room and shut the door and pray to your Father who is in secret; and your Father who sees in secret will reward you" (RSV).

John 10:9-10— "I am the door; if anyone enters by me, he will be saved, and will go in and out and find pasture. The thief comes only to steal and kill and destroy; I came that they may have life, and have it abundantly" (RSV).

John 15:11— "These things I have spoken to you, that my joy may be in you, and that your joy may be full" (RSV).

John 15:7— "If you abide in Me, and My words abide in you, ask whatever you wish, and it will be done for you" (NASB).

Revelation 22:12-13— "Behold, I am coming soon, bringing my recompense, to repay every one for what he has done. I am the Alpha and the Omega, the first and the last, the beginning and the end" (RSV).

Revelation 22:20— "He who testifies to these things says, 'Surely I am coming soon.'" (RSV) Amen. Come, Lord Jesus!

In my ministry as pastor with many major decisions to make, the promises that have been very important to me have been those involving divine guidance.

Proverbs 3:5-6 — "Trust in the Lord with all thine heart; and lean not unto thine own understanding. In all thy ways acknowledge him, and he shall direct thy paths."

Psalms 32:8 — "I will instruct thee and teach thee in the way which thou shalt go: I will guide thee with mine eye."

In thinking about guidance Psalm 23 is my favorite psalm. "The Lord is my shepherd." Thank God, I have a *guiding Shepherd*!

In the victory of Easter...

IV. We see a divine seal of credibility.

The establishment of credibility is one of the most important benefits of Easter. For this Easter sermon, I would like to list for you several credible seals which result from the victory of Easter. These seals are important validations of Christianity.

A. The resurrection provided a seal of credibility for the *existence* of our living Christ.

Despite the many attempts to disprove, deny, and destroy the fact of the resurrection of Jesus Christ; despite the fact the devil would like to destroy our belief in the resurrection; the truth remains — the resurrection is not a myth. The body was not stolen. It is not a vision of an imaginative mind. This was not a fictitious rumor.

Let us look at the proofs of His resurrection found primarily in the Gospels.
    1. The fact of an empty grave
    2. The transformation of the disciples as a result of the resurrection
    3. The birth of the Christian church
    4. The conversion of Saul of Tarsus
    5. Christ was seen by a group of over 500 people.

The apostle John had a vision of Christ some sixty years

later on the island of Patmos. Jesus spoke to John: "I am he that liveth, and was dead; and behold, I am alive for evermore..." Revelation 1:18.

It is a well attested, credible fact. Jesus Christ was dead for three days—then He left the tomb! He is risen—He is alive forevermore! The grave is empty! Thank God for our living Christ. Hallelujah! In prayer I just heard from Him this morning. Christ is alive!

B. The resurrection put a seal of credibility on our *preaching*.

It is interesting to read what Paul had to say to the Corinthians involving the resurrection. "And if Christ be not risen, then is our preaching vain, ...and we are found false witnesses of God" (I Corinthians 15:14-15).

The fact remains if Christ did not rise from the dead, all our preaching would be useless. What we have to say would be no more important than some babbling philosopher—some empty prattle. What kind of joy would one have standing in a sacred pulpit and preaching a gospel of a dead Christ?

The Lord said, "Go ye therefore, and teach all nations, ...and, lo, I am with you always, even unto the end of the world" (Matthew 28:19-20). But how could He go with us to the end of the world if He is dead?

But our preaching is not in vain! Friends, our message is different from other world religions. Our founder is not in a grave. You can find the grave of Mohammed and Buddha. But the Author of this book is still alive. Our message overflows with hope. It has the seal of credibility upon it. Let us determine to share this message with others.

C. The resurrection put a seal of credibility upon our *faith*.

"And if Christ be not raised, your faith is vain; ye are

yet in your sins" (I Corinthians 15:17). The resurrection of Jesus Christ gives authenticity to the Christian faith. The fact of His resurrection makes the teaching of Christ credible. Christ said, "Fear not; I am the first and the last: I am he that liveth, and was dead; and, behold, I am alive for evermore..." (Revelation 1:17-18). Without any doubt we can believe what Christ has done, what He has said, what He has promised.

Not only would preaching be worthless and your faith meaningless if Christ is still in the grave, notice the apostle goes on to say in I Corinthians 15:14, "And ... your faith is vain." That is, you are trusting something that does not deserve your trust. Who wants to put faith in Jesus if Jesus did not have the ability to do what He said He would do?

Jesus remains the only figure in history who died and rose from the dead by His own power. His grave clothes remained, but His body was gone. The massive stone was rolled away, but the tomb was empty. The resurrection of Jesus Christ was one of the most revolutionary events in human history. It is the greatest demonstration of power the world has ever witnessed. It is this power which can set humanity free from sin. It is resurrection power which enables us to have daily victory over the taunts and trappings of the enemy.

The resurrection gives validity to our faith. You can trust Jesus! Christ will do what He said He will do. Lidie H. Edmunds in her Easter hymn says it this way:

> My faith has found a resting place,
> Not in device nor creed;
> I trust the Ever-living One,
> His wounds for me shall plead.
> I need no other argument,
> I need no other plea,
> It is enough that Jesus died,
> And that He died for me.

In the victory of Easter…

V. We see life beyond the grave.

We are going to conclude this Easter sermon by calling your attention to one more resurrection benefit. We cannot overlook what awaits every Christian beyond this life. Death does not end it all. The prospect of immortality is the greatest hope of every believer. Eternal life is the outworking of the resurrection. Jesus conquered death, hell and the grave.

Easter dispels the fear of death.

"O death, where is thy sting? O grave, where is thy victory?" (I Corinthians 15:55).

"But thanks be to God, which giveth us the victory through our Lord Jesus Christ" (I Corinthians 15:57).

"I am he that liveth, and was dead; and, behold, I am alive for evermore, Amen; and have the keys of hell and of death" (Revelation 1:18).

Now that He lives, you and I shall live. "Jesus said to her (Martha), I am the Resurrection and the Life. Whoever believes in Me, although he may die, yet he shall live" (John 11:25 AMPC).

One of these glad and glorious mornings, the dead in Christ will hear the shout of victory.

They will hear the summons calling them to come up higher. Gravitation will lose its grip. We will ascend to meet Christ in the skies. We will have immortal, glorified bodies.

The daylight hours will never fade. The flowers will forever bloom.

The waters of the river of life flow unceasingly from the throne of God.

The tree of life bears its fruit continually. Sorrow, sickness, disappointments and death never enter.

It is the land of eternal bliss where the celestial choir sings its eternal praises to the Lamb of God.

This is the outworking of Christ's resurrection. He is the first fruit—we will be the harvest. As followers of the Lamb, we share in His victory.

One should have a heart of overflowing praise when reflecting upon the triumphant blessings of Christ's resurrection. This is more than life beyond the grave. The victory of Easter is the greatest victory in all the world. Christ was triumphant over Satan, sin and death. This magnanimous act offers us new life, living hope, fresh faith and a dynamic power.

> I serve a risen Savior;
> He's in the world today.
> I know that He is living,
> Whatever men may say.
> I see His hand of mercy;
> I hear His voice of cheer;
> And just the time I need Him
> He's always near.
> He lives, He lives,
> Christ Jesus lives today!
>
> —Alfred Ackley

Pentecost Sunday

6
THE MEANING OF PENTECOST
Acts 2:12

IN MINISTRY, IN THINKING about those special days on our church calendar, one cannot overlook the importance of Pentecost Sunday. When you think about it, I wonder if we are giving attention to the subject of Pentecost as we should. We give a lot of attention to certain birthdays, but there is not a whole lot of attention given to the birthday of the Christian church.

Today, we make much of the birth of Christ and well we should—although I am not sure that Jesus was born on December 25. Many sermons have been preached concerning the birth of Christ. But how many sermons have been preached concerning the birthday of the church?

Some may be startled when they first learn that there was a time in the Christian church when more was made of the anniversary of Pentecost than there was of Christmas. Again we are not down playing the importance of Christmas. Christmas represents the invasion of God in human form. Christmas is God coming into human history.

We celebrate the resurrection of Jesus and well we should. Easter puts a seal of completion to the sacrificial work of the Cross. But we must not overlook the importance of Pentecost. Without the outpouring of God's Spirit at Pentecost, all the previous events would have lost their significance for humanity's salvation. Without Pentecost there would have been no New Testament church. Without the day of Pentecost Christianity would have shriveled up into a little Jewish cult and died. It would have never crossed the boundaries of Jerusalem. It would have never reached out, touching the market places of the Roman Empire.

Let us begin with a little history. Pentecost was a popular Jewish festival that took place fifty days after the Feast of the Passover. The Jewish people gathered from various provinces of the Roman Empire to attend this feast. Some who gathered were men of deep piety. Some were proselytes of the Jewish faith. Fifteen different languages could have been spoken on the streets of Jerusalem that day.

But this Pentecost was different. What the people saw and heard on this day was not an everyday occurrence. They witnessed a mysterious event. There were mysterious sounds and sights. There was the sound like the rushing of a violent wind. There were flames of fire which settled above the heads of individuals. The crowd was astonished at the reality of this phenomenon. They were bewildered because each nationality heard the men speak in their own language. Being amazed, the people cried out, "What is the meaning of all this?"

Twenty centuries of church history have now passed since that day. But it is still an important question to ask. It is amazing the amount of ignorance and misunderstanding that still exists involving this wonderful event. There are aspects of Pentecost that today need to be repeated in our lives and churches.

For this Pentecost Sunday as a key phrase for this message, I would like to use three words found in Acts 2:12: "What meaneth this?" With the guidance of the Spirit, what can we learn today about the meaning of Pentecost? What happened at Pentecost?

For one thing...

I. Pentecost means the *fulfillment of a promise*.

As already mentioned, it is fascinating to think of all the unusual things that took place on this day. But what is most meaningful in this Pentecost occasion is there came a distinct fulfillment of a divine promise. Our Heavenly Father kept His word. Luke 24:49 says, "And, behold, I send the promise of my Father upon you: but tarry ye in the city of Jerusalem, until ye be endued with power from on high." Acts 1:4 says, "...But wait for the promise of the Father, which, saith he, ye have heard of me." Acts 2:33 says you shall receive from the Father "the promise of the Holy Ghost."

In effect, the word to those believers in the upper room was this: "Don't you believers leave this place. Don't leave until you receive the promise of the Father."

The disciples tarried. The promise became fulfilled. God poured out His Spirit upon them—moments never to be forgotten! It was the Father's obligation to fulfill the promise. And that is precisely what happened at Pentecost. Our heavenly Father always keeps His word.

By the way, this gift of the Holy Spirit was no little promise out of a promise box. This became a turning point in redemptive history. They were promised that something would happen, and it happened! The Christian Church was born.

- 120 people experienced a mighty baptism of the Holy Spirit.
- They were all filled with His presence and power.
- Their eyes were kindled with celestial fire.

- Their whole being pulsated with new life.

And with boldness and confidence their tongues began to speak the praises of the Lord. Previous to this, their tongues were either silent or stammering and stuttering. But not now! What a change!

Let us look at this promise. In our relationships we often use this word *promise*. What is a promise? The dictionary tells us that the word *promise* "is a pledge that we are going to do something." "It's giving us reasons why we should expect something." "I promise you that I will do this. I promise you that I will do that." But as human beings we do not always keep our word.

I will never forget how disappointed I was when a friend of mind forgot his promise. Some time ago this good brother of mine asked me if I would come to his church for a revival meeting. He gave me the dates, and he wrote them down himself in my own Day-Timer.

I was to come to his place the morning of the start of the revival. I generally check ahead, but I assumed everything was okay. The time arrived. That morning I called ahead, "Brother, just letting you know, I will soon be arriving in your town. Where do you want me to stop? I am looking forward to a good time together."

I will never forget my friend's reply. "O my soul, O my Brother Pierpoint, I forgot our dates. In fact we just finished our fall revival. O Brother Pierpoint, I am so sorry."

It was a long journey traveling from Florida to Ohio for no purpose.

It seems that some people may break their promises as often as they keep them. I am aware that my own record is not perfect. Just ask my wife. But what an encouragement it is to know our heavenly Father has never and will never forget His promises. He did not break His promise with His disciples, and He will not with us. We can depend on His promises! God keeps His word.

Before leaving this point, there are several interesting

truths that should be mentioned involving this promise.

A. It was a promise *spoken of by the Father*.

"But the Comforter, which is the Holy Ghost, whom the Father will send in my name, he shall teach you all things..." (John 14:26). Actually, the inference in this expression, "the promise of the Father," is found a number of times in the Scriptures.

"For I will pour water upon him that is thirsty, and floods upon the dry ground: I will pour my spirit upon thy seed, and my blessing upon thine offspring" (Isaiah 44:3).

"And I will put my spirit within you, and cause you to walk in my statutes, and ye shall keep my judgments, and do them" (Ezekiel 36:27).

Listen to the prophet Joel as he speaks of the Father's promise 800 years prior to Pentecost: "...I will pour out my spirit upon all flesh; and your sons and your daughters shall prophecy, your old men shall dream dreams, your young men shall see visions: and also upon the servants and upon the handmaids in those days will I pour out my spirit" (Joel 2:28,29).

B. It was a promise *spoken of frequently*.

For the greater part of His ministry, Christ rarely mentioned the Spirit. On the eve of His passion, however, He spoke of the Spirit's coming with an amazing fullness. It seemed like it was the Master's chief concern. Listen.

"But the Comforter, which is the Holy Ghost, whom the Father will send in my name, he shall teach you all things..." (John 14:26).

"...It is expedient for you that I go away: for if I go not away, the Comforter will not come unto you; but if I depart, I will send him unto you" (John 16:7).

Christ's last words to His disciples were these: "And,

behold, I send the promise of my Father upon you..." (Luke 24:49).

The third factor about this promise...

C. It is a promise *spoken to the faithful.*

Although the promise had been long delayed, their faith did not waver. They were all there—120 of them—waiting obediently to the command of Christ. God does not pour out His blessings on the disobedient. The Father's promises cannot be fulfilled unless as children we are obedient to His will. Had the assembled gathering failed to wait in submissive obedience, there might have been no Pentecost.

I am thinking of the old song we used to sing...

> They were in an upper chamber,
> They were all with one accord,
> When the Holy Ghost descended
> As was promised by the Lord.
>
> Yes, this old-time power was given
> To our fathers who were true;
> This is promised to believers,
> And we all may have it, too.
>
> O Lord, send the power just now...
> And baptize everyone.

In meditating on the meaning of Pentecost, we might ask, "What was the promise that was fulfilled?" Not only was there the fulfillment of a promise...

II. At Pentecost there came an *enduement of a power.*

"And, behold, I send the promise of my Father upon you: but tarry ye in the city of Jerusalem, until ye be endued with power from on high" (Luke 24:49). "But ye shall receive power, after that the Holy Ghost is come upon you…" (Acts 1:8).

What can we learn about the nature of this power that was promised?

A. We have revealed for us the *source of this power*.

There was nothing human about the power manifested on that occasion. The source of their power came from above. It was divine. It came from none other than the person of the Holy Spirit.

We need to keep this truth in mind. As we face the trials and battles of life, we constantly need the help of the Holy Spirit. For the disciples the courage they had, the power they demonstrated, the joy they experienced, the victory that was theirs all came from the Holy Spirit.

And by the way, their need for help not only happened at Pentecost, it happened many other times in their lives and in their service. Humanly speaking, no matter what you think you can accomplish, however you think you can handle your problems, your source of human strength may not be sufficient. You are no match for the enemy of your soul. As He was their source of power of that day, He is our source of power today. We cannot make it without the guiding, guarding influences of the Holy Spirit. How important it is to keep filled with the Spirit. (Ephesians 5:18)

B. We have revealed for us the *strength of this power*.

Let us examine the strength of this power. Have you ever stopped to think how ordinary, how limited this little group of disciples were? They were not leaders. They were untaught, unlettered men—weak faltering men. But look at what happened. At Pentecost these assembled believers were empowered, emboldened to become what they were not capable of being before Pentecost. They fearlessly demonstrated a strength that robbed them of their fears, weaknesses, their failures. They demonstrated a power that was liberating. The word *power* comes from the word *dunamis* from which we derive the word *dynamite*—unlimited power. Who can measure the strength of divine energy? There are no limitations to God's power. All this happened at Pentecost 2,000 years ago, but the strength of His power has never diminished. Pentecost can be perpetuated. The reality of God's presence and power can be ours today.

C. We have revealed for us the *service of this power*.

In your Bible you have a book called "Acts—The Acts of the Apostles." But really it contains the acts of the Holy Spirit. As we read through the book of Acts, starting with Pentecost we find a number of different forms of activities and services ascribed to the Holy Spirit. What did the Holy Spirit do? And what can He do for us today?

1. There is the *caring* service of the Holy Spirit.

At Pentecost the Holy Spirit came to take the place of Christ. During His days on earth, Jesus was their companion. He cared for them. He stood by them. He wept with them. Being human, however, His presence was limited. He could not be in two locations at once. There were times the disciples were alone to face the stormy seas of life. After Pentecost the Holy Spirit was "one called alongside to help."

2. There is the *counseling* service of the Holy Spirit.

I am thinking of the words found in John 14:26: "But the Comforter, which is the Holy Ghost, whom the Father will send in my name, he shall teach you all things, and bring all things to your remembrance, whatsoever I have said unto you." "Howbeit when he, the Spirit of truth, is come, he will guide you into all truth…" (John

16:13). I do not think these promises were just for the disciples. Oh, how I thank God for the guiding service of the Holy Spirit that we can experience today.

3. There is the *correcting* service of the Holy Spirit.

As disturbing as it may seem, I thank God for this activity of the Holy Spirit. The book of Acts is filled with countless stories of the Holy Spirit controlling and correcting those leaders of the early church. Sometimes those corrective efforts were a little painful. Breaking with tradition, Peter had a little difficult time sharing the gospel to the Gentiles.

But let us not be too hard on Peter. May we in the current of this modern age be attentive to checks and corrections of the Holy Spirit. God knows the subtle dangers we face. He knows the path we should follow. Victorious living comes when there is full submission to the Spirit's correcting control. Our desires, impulses and behaviors humanly speaking may need the corrective, constructive ministry of the Spirit.

4. There is a *cleansing* service of the Holy Spirit.

At Pentecost did not the Holy Spirit come in cleansing power? The cleansing activity of the Spirit must not be overlooked. There is some theological discussion over this aspect of Pentecost. However, Scripture records in Acts 15:8-9: "And God, which knoweth the hearts, bare them witness, giving them the Holy Ghost, even as He did unto us; and put no difference between us and them, purifying their hearts by faith." Would this not mean that Pentecost involved the obtainment of a purity?

Let me remind you, these men were followers of Christ—they were disciples of Christ. But these men needed a work of purity in their hearts. Their hearts were divided. There were the remnants of self that were dominant in their life. They had a party spirit. There were the roots of a fleshly disposition. At times they demonstrated the elements of selfishness, pride, self-seeking, cowardice. They were not controlled by a fullness of love. Whatever your thoughts may be on this baptism of the Spirit, the biblical fact is that at Pentecost a purifying change did come in their lives. There was the service of cleansing.

Is there another meaning which we should examine? Pentecost means the *fulfillment of a promise*. Pentecost means the *enduement of a power*.

III. Pentecost means the *encouragement of a Presence*.

In looking at what happened at Pentecost, there are several other encouraging ministries of the Holy Spirit which might be mentioned. They should not be omitted.

A. Pentecost means the encouragement of a *continuing Presence*.

Jesus was informing His disciples that He was going away. He had to leave them. Obviously, they were sad, brokenhearted. I am sure the disciples were saying something like this, "Master, we will be like orphans with no support or guidance."

But the Master quickly replied, "I am going to send you another Comforter."

Can you hear the disciples talking back? "How long will He abide with us? Thou hast been with us only a little while, and now Thou art going away. How long will the other Comforter of whom Thou hast spoken abide with us?"

And, oh, how their hearts must have been cheered by the announcement, "He shall abide with you for ever." (John 14:16) Pentecost means the encouragement of an abiding Presence, a continuing Presence. And unless you quench the fire of the Spirit, unless you are saying no to the authority of the Spirit in your life, there will be the continual indwelling of His presence. There will be no departure of His guiding hand over the road of life. There will be no lifting of His abiding, cheering Presence from the region of your soul.

It matters not where you might be or what your circumstances might be. According to the promise, the presence of the Holy Spirit will be with us until the end of time. I can still hear Dr. Steve Herron share these lines at the close of one of his great sermons: "It's been almost 1900 years since that first Pentecost. I would like to tell you something: the blessed Holy Spirit is still here. Hallelujah! He hasn't taken a day off during all this time.
- His Presence is still available.
- His Presence is still capable.
- His Presence is still doing all He has ever done.
- He has come to abide!"

B. Pentecost means the encouragement of a *comforting Presence*.

At Pentecost the Holy Spirit came to be their *Comforter*. John 16:7 says: "Nevertheless I tell you the truth; It is expedient for you (It is best for you; it is profitable for you.) that I go away: for if I go not away, the Comforter will not come unto you; but if I depart, I will send him unto you."

The word *comfort* is rich in meaning. It means "one who is called alongside to help, one who assists, one to bring aid, one who will be with us through all our trials."

What an encouragement it can bring to our hearts to think that one of the frequent titles for the Holy Spirit is the word *Comforter*. This seems to be a favorite title for the Holy Spirit, and it is a beautiful one.

Let us note the imminent interest and concern which Christ shared for the coming of the Spirit upon the disciples. Observe the confidence He had in the person and presence of the Holy Spirit to meet the comforting needs of those wobbling, faltering disciples.

1. Christ was confident of the fact that the Holy Spirit

could fill His place fully and completely.
2. Christ was confident of the fact that the Holy Spirit could meet every need of this little group of disciples.
3. Christ was confident of the fact that the Holy Spirit's presence would be completely adequate to protect, to guide, to instruct, to inspire and to provide their need for comfort.

C. Pentecost means the encouragement of a *conquering Presence*.

There was an overcoming power that came to those at Pentecost. The doors of the upper room were flung open. Gone were those marks of hesitancy and fear. Baptized with a spirit of courage, those disciples went out on the balcony enlivened. They marched through the streets equipped by His Presence. With His indwelling power they spoke the word with boldness. (Acts 4:31) Their timidity and fear were gone. The disciples went into the temple and fearlessly declared to the multitude, "Jesus is Lord. Jesus is the prince of life. Jesus is the Messiah."

In many ways today's circumstances differ from those on the day of Pentecost. However, the Spirit's presence was not just for those early Christians. It is our conviction that the conquering presence of the Holy Spirit is as available to us as in any other era. There is an overcoming power that can enable us to maintain victory in our lives. Keep encouraged! We have reason to be confident even in the face of trouble. Through the Holy Spirit there is a conquering vitality promised us. Acts 1:8: "But ye shall receive power, after that the Holy Ghost is come upon you...."

As we close this message, all would agree that Pentecost made a tremendous difference in the lives of those disciples. But is Pentecost simply an historical event of centuries past? Should we try to repeat this event? No, we cannot go back to Pentecost dispensationally and expect a repeated occurrence. This outpouring of the Holy Spirit marked the initial launching of the church. It is not possible to turn time back 2000 years and attend Pentecost. However, we can go back to Pentecost experientially.

The promise of the Father is not just for those at Pentecost. It was not just for those 120 in the upper room. The Holy Spirit which descended on the day of Pentecost filling the lives of those disciples longs to come to us today filling our own hearts and lives with His presence. Pentecost can be a living reality in our lives in the twenty-first century.

He who was central at Pentecost wants to be central in our church, He wants to be central in our lives and in our homes. Effective ministry in our churches does not depend on human skills or human enterprises. For victorious living in our individual lives, there is the need for the fullness of the Spirit. We simply cannot make it without the Spirit's supernatural power and presence. The message is relevant today.

Ephesians 5:18 in the International Standard Version says, "...Keep on being filled with the Spirit." How essential it is that we stay connected. Our need is not for cloven tongues of fire or the sound of rushing wind. However, the prayer of our hearts could be expressed in the text of this timeless hymn:

Breathe on me, Breath of God,
Fill me with life anew,
That I may love what Thou dost love,
And do what Thou wouldst do.

Breathe on me, Breath of God,
'Til I am wholly Thine,
Until this earthly part of me
Glows with Thy fire divine.

MOTHER'S DAY

7
QUALITIES OF AN EXEMPLARY MOTHER
Proverbs 31

As I thought about the message for Mother's Day, I wondered what could be said about mother that has not already been said. In honor of mother what more could I add? It is true there are various opinions about what a mother should be like in our current day. Some of these views could be quite fashionable. With this in mind, I think it is important to find out what the Scripture has to say about mother.

The verses of the last chapter of Proverbs constitute one of the most descriptive tributes of womanhood to be found in Holy Scriptures. While the tribute is a part of Old Testament culture, there are timeless principles here. For our Mother's Day service, I would like to single out several of these praiseworthy qualities. In this day of broken homes, dysfunctional families, and illicit relationships, a study of Solomon's ideal mother can be vastly important. These virtues can be used today. Actually, the woman he describes may be not only a mother or a wife—even single ladies could be included. The principles are the same.

What kind of woman does Solomon consider worthy of praise?

I. She is a *virtuous woman*.

Solomon starts out by saying, "Who can find a virtuous woman? For her price (her worth) is far above rubies" (verse 10). The writer closes this chapter by saying, "…Beauty is vain: but a woman that feareth the Lord, she shall be praised" (verse 30).

Today many women believe Proverbs 31 does not really apply to our modern lives. But we believe there are truths here which are applicable and needful. God's Word stands the test of time. The qualities spoken of here are not outdated. In using the word *virtuous*, Solomon is not just talking about moral excellence. He is talking about the timeless virtues of godly character. He lists for us various character strengths. The world honors people for their looks, their beauty, their money and perhaps some particular talent. But God honors people for their character rather than facial charm.

A virtuous woman serves God with all her heart, mind and soul. She seeks His will for her life and follows His ways. Her conduct is governed by her fear of the Lord, not by what others think. (Proverbs 31:29-31, Matthew 22:37, John 14:15, Psalm 119:15) The price of a virtuous woman "is far above rubies."

What kind of woman does Solomon consider worthy of praise? She is not only a virtuous woman…

II. She is a *vigorous worker*.

Solomon gives us another description of her character. There is nothing lazy about this woman. There is no idleness or slothfulness found in her life. I like what Solomon says in verse 27: "She…eateth not the bread of idleness."

I am amazed at the long list of motherly duties found in this chapter. She sacrificed a great deal of time, energy and effort tending sheep, drawing water, and making clothing and tapestries. But she did so willingly and cheerfully. She gathered in the crops and took pleasure in her part of the whole process which put food on the table. This virtuous woman loved her family, and her love was demonstrated in deeds—in hours of labor and toil. In modern language she did not sit around watching TV all day.

The illustration I am about to give may sound unrealistic, but it is a real-life story of a truly vigorous mother of a former day. This lady was a mother of nine children. She had a big garden from which she canned her vegetables. In those days there was no such thing as freezing food. Everything had to be canned. When they butchered the pig, this meat was also canned. She made nine loaves of bread twice a week. She made her own sauerkraut. In the basement you would find barrels of apples that had been picked. Before this family obtained electricity, they burned kerosene lamps that had to be cleaned frequently. She was a good seamstress who made clothes for her family. She even made gloves for her children out of old socks. As you can see, this mother did not have any time to post her activities on Facebook or any time for recreational activity. By the way, this godly mother saw that her children were made ready for church every Sunday. Today we may not quite have this type of schedule, but Solomon wisely said that a model mother "eateth not the bread of idleness." You cannot be lazy and be a model mother.

What kind of woman does Solomon consider worthy of praise? She is not only a *virtuous woman* and a *vigorous worker*...

III. She is a *valuable wife*.

In this chapter, with rare skill and deep insight Solomon delineates the work of a good wife. This is reflected in terms of service to her husband. Few passages in the Bible so clearly set out the scope of the ministry of a married woman as this one. I like his climactic statement mentioned in verse 12: "She will do him good…all the days of her life."

Here is the question before us. What does a good wife do? What makes her so valuable?

A. A good wife will *compliment* her husband.

She will do him good verbally by using words to praise and reverence him. She knows how to build his soul and comfort his heart. She is not a brawling, contentious, complaining companion. A good wife is not a "whiner." She does not nag her husband. Proverbs 21:9 says: "It is better to dwell in a corner of the housetop, than with a brawling (complaining) woman in a wide house." (Proverbs 27:15) And Proverbs 21:19 states: "It is better to dwell in the wilderness, than with a contentious and an angry woman." A good wife does not seek to compete with her husband. She seeks to compliment him.

B. A good wife is *committed* to her husband.

1. It is a commitment of love.

She thinks the world of him. Her love for him is never lost. "She will do him good…all the days of her life" (verse 12). On his birthday, on Facebook you should read how she brags on him. She supports his values and goals. She is committed to making him look good. She irons his shirts, picks up his clothes, mends his socks, and cooks what he likes. On and on goes the list of service to her loved one. You might say it this way, "Her husband is what he is because of what she is."

2. But above all, it is a commitment of prayer.

Her husband's welfare is promoted by a praying wife. The word *prayer* is not directly mentioned in this chapter.

But there is a reason why her husband trusts her (verse 11). And there is a reason why her children arise and call her blessed (verse 28). You cannot leave out the value of prayer and look well to the ways of your household (verse 27). You cannot be God-fearing and live a prayer-less life (verse 30). I thank God for Mother's prayers.

C. A good wife *counsels* her husband.

When God designed the roles of husband and wife, he fashioned the wife as a helpmate for her husband. Among other gifts, God often grants the wife an alertness and discernment He may not initially give to the husband. God said, "It is not good that the man should be alone; I will make him an help meet for him" (Genesis 2:18). A wise husband will listen to the guarding cautions of his wife. She may not always be wrong. I confess my wife has been a great help to me in this area. Patience is not one of my virtues. Sometimes I move ahead without thinking. Thank God, I often stopped and listened to my wife. "She openeth her mouth with wisdom" (verse 26).

What kind of woman does Solomon consider worthy of praise? She is not only a *virtuous woman*, a *vigorous worker*, and a *valuable wife*...

IV. She is a *vibrant witness*.

In no small way she shares her loving care. Let us see where this caring witness is demonstrated.

A. Her life is a vibrant witness *to those in need*.

"She stretcheth out her hand to the poor; yea, she reacheth forth her hands to the needy" (verse 20). "...In her tongue is the law of kindness" (verse 26). Yes, her hands are busy with household chores. But more than that, she is willing to go beyond her routine duties to help those who are in need. Those hands are busy, caring, helping others. Her good deeds are witnessed by many. Her character is observable. In her community she is known for her compassionate concern making others speak well of her. They see kindness demonstrated.

In my congregation, as a pastor it was always a joy to see various mothers constantly going out of their way to help others. Their homes were often open to visitors. They took special interest in those who were in need. Their prayer list involved a number of unsaved people. They were vibrant examples of thoughtfulness and kindness.

B. Her life is a vibrant witness *to her children.*

She nurtures her children with the love of Christ, disciplines them with care and wisdom, and trains them in the way they should go. "Her children arise up, and call her blessed; her husband also, and he praiseth her" (verse 28). (Proverbs 22:6) There cannot be any greater reward or joy than to have your children come and say, "Mom, I thank you for the wonderful memories we have of you — memories of your love for us, your care for us, your prayers for us. Mom, we thank you for your life."

This is Mother's Day. We thank God for these qualities of a virtuous mother listed in this chapter. It has been an interesting study. In closing I want to give a "bouquet of praise" to all our mothers who are exhibiting or striving to exhibit these virtues in their everyday life. In this day of broken homes and dysfunctional families, this study of God's ideal of womanhood should be vastly important. We are also grateful for our singles whose lives are also examples of godly living.

Father's Day

8
PRIORITIES OF A GOOD FATHER
1 Corinthians 16:13-14

As a pastor it has been my practice across the years to take advantage of those special days that are set apart in the calendar of the church. Father's Day is one of them.

I do appreciate the recognition and honor we give our mothers on Mother's Day. We often do it with flying colors. Sometimes we even get downright sentimental. But poor old dad hardly gets a passing nod. The emphasis of this message is on the important role of fatherhood. I would like to zero in on our dads and grandads.

First let me give you something on the lighter side. I want to give you nine reasons why it is great to be a man.
1. Phone conversations are over in thirty seconds flat.
2. You can "do" your nails with a pocketknife.
3. You can comb your hair in thirty seconds—especially if you are baldheaded.
4. You can leave the motel bed unmade without feeling guilty.
5. Three pairs of shoes are more than enough.
6. You are unable to see the wrinkles in your clothes.

7. You do not have to carry pocketbooks around with you. One wallet is enough.
8. Your hands are not made for doing dishes.
9. You can do Christmas shopping for twenty-five relatives on December 24 in forty-five minutes.

It is great to be a man!

A number of years ago the United States Marine Corps put on an advertising campaign to encourage more men to enlist. Do you remember the Marines' ad? "We're looking for a few good men."

Incidentally, one young lady in her vanishing twenties paused to read the poster. With a sigh she was heard to say, "I can beat that. All I want is just one good man."

But more than maids, more than Marines, and more than the military, this is the need of communities. This is the need of the churches. This is the need of our homes. We need some good men! We need good fathers.

In the last chapter of 1 Corinthians, the apostle gives a cluster of final instructions and greetings. Right in the middle of all of this, Paul gives us a little sermon in a nutshell. He inserts a short but interesting statement about how men should live. There are just two verses, but they are powerful. First Corinthians 16:13-14 says: "Be on your guard, stand firm in the faith, live like men, be strong! Let everything that you do be done in love" (Phillips).

And while these are some of the final words to the church of Corinth, yet I find in this text perfect words for a good Father's Day sermon.

Looking at our text, I am choosing these words as a title, "The Priorities of a Good Father." In thinking about building strong homes, strong men, strong fathers and strong churches, the challenge here is timeless. The instruction is both needful and helpful.

What can we learn from these verses? There are several challenging commands—imperatives—found in our text. In these verses we find first of all…

I. The priority of *alert living*.

"Be on your guard, stand firm in the faith" (I Corinthians 16:13 Phillips).

The apostle tells us that we should be on guard. We are to keep our eyes open. Be alert. Be vigilant.

The church of Corinth desperately needed this exhortation. There were many glaring evils and weaknesses developing in the Corinthian church—dissensions, heresies, friction, and even immorality. Is it any wonder that Paul exhorted them to be watchful and alert?

The reminder is not just for the Corinthians of that day. The need for alertness is still important. Today even in the best of churches, even with the best of people, there is still a need to be on guard. We live in a very wicked society. The pressures to conform to the spirit of this age are subtle and serious. We need to be on the alert.

But in this message today, we are not thinking so much about those dark, deliberate, outward failures found in the Corinthian church, I am thinking of perils of another type—perils that are often overlooked—common perils that all Christians face. And our fathers are no exception. Of all people, dads, you are a prime target for the devil. Be on your guard involving these common dangers.

A. Guard against the peril of *misplaced priorities*.

Dad, as a husband and father what are your priorities? Have you ever thought about what activities are most important in your life? The fact is we all live in a very busy world. Between work, home, church, community, we do not have a whole lot of time left on our hands. Sometimes we feel overwhelmed. Be alert! There is a subtle danger here. In the midst of the busyness of life, it is easy to lose sight of the priorities that should guide us in our responsibilities—priorities to our wives, children and most importantly to our Lord. Some homes are a minor tragedy, not because of some wickedness or terrible sin, but because biblical goals for the home were never made clear or never established.

1. In discussing our priorities, the very first item is your relationship with Christ.

"For to me to live is Christ..." (Philippians 1:21). The controlling ambition of your life is to please Christ. There is no higher goal than this.

In pursuing this goal, do not overlook the importance of prayer. "Praying always with all prayer and supplication in the Spirit..." (Ephesians 6:18). Dad, what priority do you give your prayer life? One of the dangers we face is that our lives can be so cluttered with a busy schedule the voice of God is drowned out.

Our relationship to Christ is maintained and strengthened not only through prayer, but also from the study of God's Word. Again, there is nothing more important, no goal any higher, than seeking to live the Christ-life. Fathers, guard your commitment to following Christ. Nothing is more important than this.

In the New Testament it is interesting to note how many times the commands *watching* and *prayer* are joined together. "Take ye heed, watch and pray: for ye know not when the time is" (Mark 13:33). "Always maintain the habit of prayer: be both alert and thankful as you pray" (Colossians 4:2 Phillips).

2. The second priority involves your relationship with your family.

"And, ye fathers, provoke not your children to wrath: but bring them up in the nurture and admonition of the Lord" (Ephesians 6:4). Be alert! How important is your family? As a pastor I was guilty. There were times I was so taken up with the concerns of the church that my time with the family was missing. How much time do we spend with our children? Should this concern not be a priority? What value do you place on saving your family? Outside of your own personal devotion to Christ, your time and concern for the family should be next.

It is a mistake to suppose your children automatically will be Christians simply because you profess to be a Christian. Unfortunately, you can even be a good Christian but at the same time a poor parent. Parents can exercise poor judgement, be lacking in discipline, and demonstrate critical attitudes. Perhaps the salvation of your children was not the ultimate goal in your home. Fathers, watch out for these dangers. Keep on your guard.

What are we to watch? We need not only guard against the peril of misplaced priorities, we must...

B. Guard against the peril of *materialistic goals*.

We live in a society were great emphasis is placed on the material rather than the spiritual — the immediate rather than the future. Material pursuits are often chief concerns. The philosophy of the day is live for self, enjoy yourself, get what you can get. If it is a lot of fun, it has to be right.

What priority should you place on material acquisition? It is difficult to know where to place this priority. Should making money be our first priority? It takes money to support the family. With the rising cost of living, family members sometimes have to find extra employment to make ends meet. After all bills need to be paid.

Caution is needed. There is a balance. Living a less materialistic lifestyle does not mean becoming a monk and abstaining from all of life's pleasures. It means shifting your focus on what is most important. Do you need a brand-new car? Can an older one do? Do you really need that new gun? Are your wants and needs becoming mixed up? What you desire, you really may not need. There is more to living than living for material possessions. It is not wrong to have nice things, but it is wrong when they control our lives. Your biggest concern should be more than material interests. What does a man profit if he should gain the whole world, but lose his own family or lose his own soul? (Matthew 16:26)

I will never forget an incident that took place at my church. A father came to me and said, "Pastor, we are moving to another city." I was taken back. I hated to lose this family. But worse still, I was disappointed with the thinking of my good brother when he told me why they were leaving. "Pastor, I have found a job that will give me twice the money I am making now. I can't resist the opportunity."

I turned to my dear friend and said, "Great, but what church will you be going to?" The father replied, "I don't know. We will find something, sometime. But I am not going to turn down a good paying job." I asked myself, what was important in the man's life? Was it not important to know what church his family would attend? "Pastor, I am not worried about that." What is important? "I can't afford to miss this opportunity of making more money." An example of misplaced priorities. Yes, we are exhorted to be watchful, keep alert. What are those important goals in your life?

What can we learn from these verses? Again in this text the apostle gives us another challenge. We not only have a mandate for *alert living*, we have...

II. The priority of *adult living*.

"Watch ye, stand fast in the faith, quit you like men, be strong" (1 Corinthians 16:13).

What does the apostle mean by this phrase, "quit you like men?" Essentially, as various translators put it, what the apostle is saying is this: "Act like a man." "Be an adult." "Quit acting like children." The kind of life some of these Corinthians were living was far from anything mature. In one sense the apostle is contrasting spiritual maturity with childishness. In contrast with a child, a grown man is expected to have more intelligence, wisdom, strength, self-control than a mere child.

Examine the complaint the apostle gives to this church at Corinth. He says in effect, "You Corinthians, you need to grow up. You are acting like babies." "And I, brethren, could not speak unto you as unto spiritual, but as unto carnal, even as unto babes in Christ" (I Corinthians 3:1). "…There is among you envying, and strife, and divisions…" (I Corinthians 3:3). In effect, Paul gives a similar parallel admonition in chapter thirteen: "When I was a child, I spake as a child, I understood as a child, I thought as a child: but when I became a man, I put away childish things" (verse 11). Ephesians 4:14: "That we henceforth be no more children, tossed to and fro, and carried about with every wind of doctrine…."

In essence the apostle is pointing out the need for spiritual maturity. Obviously, Paul is not talking about masculine qualities, mere human traits or physical development. He is talking about the call to biblical manhood — being an adult spiritually. The apostle is talking about conducting yourself in a specific way.

In infancy there is a selfishness, quarreling, arguments, divisions, unreconciled relationships, crying for attention. In maturity there is unity, humility, steadfastness, reconciliation, healing and of course the manifestation of the love of Christ.

I wonder if this might not be the need of our day? Confession is good for the soul. As a father I think there have been a few times in my own life I could have used a few extra doses of spiritual maturity. Every church needs mature fathers. We need men of faith, men of courage, men of spiritual strength. We do not need troublemakers; we need peacemakers.

What does spiritual maturity look like? It is the highest level of manhood developed and governed by devotion to Christ. It is a life controlled by one's desire to please Christ. "For me to live is Christ…" (Philippians 1:21). It is making choices to live by God's viewpoint rather than some human viewpoint. It is a life that looks out more for the needs of others than your own needs. It is a life that stands fast in the faith. Those who are strong in the faith are not moved by false doctrine and loose morals. Spiritual maturity is consistent, courageous living.

But, one may ask, is this kind of living possible in today's modern society? Yes! This quality of life is nothing gained by yourself. It is not a product of human effort. It comes by surrendering fully to the molding process of the Holy Spirit. Thank God, there is strength that one can have for mature living. We could not make it without the guiding, guarding influences of the Holy Spirit. This is the path that is essential to mature living. I am grateful to God for those mature fathers I have known who have demonstrated this quality of life. They did not overlook their need for adult living. They were strong in the Lord. "Watch ye, stand fast in the faith, quit you like men, be strong" (I Corinthians 16:13).

When I think of a mature father, Graham Price, my father-in-law, comes to mind. In him the ingredients of spiritual maturity were displayed. There was the characteristic of integrity. After many years of farming, my father-in- law decided to sell his farm, retire and move to a nearby town. The news went out that Graham Price had his farm up for sale. A man came by and offered Mr. Price a certain amount for the land. The two men agreed that a specific figure was what the sale price would be. A few days later another potential buyer came along and offered Mr. Price a higher figure.

The response was that a verbal commitment had been made, and he could not go back on his word. There had been nothing in writing and, had he chosen to, Mr. Price could have taken the second offer. But his word was his bond. This verbal commitment, though unofficial, cost Mr. Price thousands of dollars. His integrity, his word, kept him from doing otherwise.

In Mr. Price there was also demonstrated a spiritual commitment. He did not serve Christ out of convenience. Every time the church doors were open, he and his family were there. This involved revivals, prayer meetings, Sunday school—you name it. Only sickness would keep them from coming. Mr. Price never missed church to harvest his wheat on Sunday, even if a rainstorm was predicted. And the Lord usually "looked out for him." Although the family lived a few miles from the church, they were seldom late. Being on time was a priority. Thank God for mature fathers!

We not only have a mandate *for alert living* and *adult living*, in this verse we have...

III. The priority of *affectionate living*

We are talking about priorities of being a good father. The last command we find in our text involves the word *love*. Paul says in verse fourteen, "Let all that you do be done with love" (MEV).

In talking about affectionate living, we are talking about the quality of love as a motivating force behind mature living. Now the word *love* is perhaps the most important word in our text. However, in modern vernacular the word *love* has become a very common word which is used in many different ways. "I love that new suit he is wearing." "I love those lower gas prices." "I love those pink flowers."

In the words of our text, the apostle is not talking about this common use of love. He is not talking about sensual or shallow love. He is not talking about some passing emotion or some kind of nice feeling. He is talking about love as a dynamic force in our lives that controls our action and behavior. He is talking about love as a supreme virtue in Christian living. It brings spiritual maturity.

The Corinthian congregation desperately needed this admonition—and not just the men. They were divided and bickering with each other. Love was terribly lacking in their lives. With this in mind, in addition to these exhortations the apostle wrote a whole chapter on the subject of love. First Corinthians thirteen is one of the greatest chapters in the Bible.

There is a need for this command to be realized today. Why are there so many failed marriages? Homes are being broken up. The divorce rate is high. What is the reason for these damaged relationships? The governing influence of divine love is being lost.

While this truth about love is a message for all Christians, our focus of course is on fathers. What can our fathers learn from this truth that would be helpful?

In talking about love as seen in our text, there are two questions that come to mind.

A. What does this love do?

Affectionate living is important because of what this love does. Love is meeting the needs of others. Love is being considerate of others. Love is putting others above self. Love is giving and sacrificing for the sake of others. Love is all about others! Love is slow to lose patience. It looks the other way to build others up. It is not possessive. It does not cherish inflated ideas of its own importance. Love is kind and caring.

By the way, this kind of affection makes a good check for dads. Love keeps his firmness from becoming harsh and his strength from becoming domineering. Without love watchfulness can deteriorate into a judgmental spirit.

Without love one can become militant. This lack of love is what was happening to the Corinthian church. This can happen to us—it can happen to fathers.

There is a second question.

B. Where should this love be demonstrated?

Love is very important in community living. You do not make many friends when you are snobbish, arrogant, unfriendly. We could spend the rest of our time talking about the importance of love in church life. But more important than anything else is the demonstration of love for the family. Where love is not the foundation of a home, problems arise. Love should be seen in the home. You cannot be a good father without this quality of love.

Dad, does your wife have your love? As a husband no other human being is as important as your wife. A good husband loves, honors, and cherishes his wife in every respect. Does it need to be said? Love is the most important quality in the development of caring husbands. The apostle specifically mentions this. The Amplified Bible expressed it this way in Colossians 3:19: "Husbands, love your wives [be affectionate and sympathetic with them] and do not be harsh or bitter or resentful toward them." Be considerate and tender. The husband loves his wife above all other human beings. By the way, the demonstration of your love (or your lack of love) for your wife is setting a pattern for your sons to follow. They are learning from you how to treat their wives.

Then naturally it will follow that a father will love his children. The most important thing a father can do for his children is to love the Lord and reflect that kind of love in the home. The role of a good father is demonstrated in his affectionate concern for his children. A godly father loves his children. His behavior is guided by love.

In caring for his children, there is a need for discipline. Rearing children is challenging. Discipline is often administered without love. There is no place for an overbearing and abusive father. Discipline is much more effective when a father affirms his children frequently. No challenge rings any clearer in my mind that the command the apostle gives in Ephesians 6:4: "Fathers, do not irritate and provoke your children to anger [do not exasperate them to resentment], but rear them [tenderly] in the training and discipline and the counsel and admonition of the Lord" (AMPC). This cannot be done without love. Love is the most essential quality in the development of caring fathers!

Again the priority of a good father is seen in the time he takes with his children. A loving father spends quality time with them. He sets aside time daily or weekly to be with his children. His son's baseball game is a father's priority. A daughter's piano recital is an important family event. No matter how busy he might be, dad is there in those big moments of their lives.

Dads, do not miss the season of childhood. Those are the formative years, and there is no second chance. Children grow up so fast. Can you believe this? Bill just got his driver's permit. Mary saw her highchair up in the attic. It was hard to believe that one time she sat in that chair.

Dads, guard those spiritual times with your children. Pray with them. Pray for them. Sing with them. Daily read sections from your Bible storybook. Commend them for their good behavior. Remember this—your love for Christ is not only seen in the church, it is best seen in the home.

In closing as a mandate for men, let us review the challenge of our text. The priorities of a good father have been emphasized. A good dad knows something about *alert living*, *adult living* and *affectionate living*.

Are you manifesting the true maturity God wants of

you? Are you seeking to grow in the grace, knowledge, and love of God? It is not a mere doctrine that makes one mature. It is living the love of God in your heart, words and deeds.

Fathers, let me encourage you in the importance of your role. Be a strong leader, a loving role model, and a spiritual guide for your family. May the love of your family be showered upon you on Father's Day because you have earned their respect and affection.

I would like to close this message with a poem given to me by my daughter Paula. I treasure that Father's Day card which expressed her love for her dad.

> My Dad is an Example
>
> There are many examples to follow in life,
> Many men who are deserving of praise.
> Whether doctors or lawyers or soldiers of war,
> They've given in so many ways.
> But of all the men who have accomplished it all—
> Of all the great leaders we've had,
> Not one will ever begin to compare
> With the example I've had in my dad.
> He's taught me values,
> He's raised me with love
> He's always shown me his respect.
> And though his name many never appear in bright lights,
> He's one man you'd never forget.
> My dad is a leader, my pattern for life,
> And on him I can surely depend.
> For I know he will be there with arms open wide
> To be my example, my friend.
>
> —Amy Matayo

Independence Sunday

9
THE FREEDOM CHRIST BRINGS

"...Where the Spirit of the Lord is, there is liberty" (II Corinthians 3:17).

"And ye shall know the truth, and the truth shall make you free" (John 8:32).

"If the Son therefore shall make you free, ye shall be free indeed" (John 8:36).

THE FOURTH OF JULY IS A GOOD TIME to think about the subject of freedom. For us it marks the birthday of our country. It was on this date in 1776 that a charter of freedom was adopted—the Declaration of Independence. The celebration of our nation's birthday is really a celebration of freedom. In whatever way we may celebrate this occasion, as Americans we need to pause and thank God for the freedom we enjoy in our country. There are places in this world where this freedom is not found. This could also become the case in our beloved USA.

While our national freedom is precious, our freedom in Christ is of infinite worth. The importance of this subject is seen in the frequent references to this theme in the Bible. It is interesting to note the number of song writers using this theme. The great hymn writer Charles Wesley was undoubtedly moved by his freedom in Christ when in 1738 he penned this stanza:

> Long my imprisoned spirit lay
> Fast bound in sin and nature's night;
> Thine eye diffused a quickening ray,
> I woke, the dungeon flamed with light;
> My chains fell off, my heart was free;
> I rose, went forth, and followed Thee.

The saving truth Jesus speaks of in John 8:36 shows us the freedom Christ brings. "If the Son therefore shall make you free, ye shall be free indeed." The people to whom the Master was speaking, even though they started believing on Christ, did not understand the kind of freedom Jesus was talking about.

Those Jews were very deceived concerning liberty! They thought because they were descendants of Abraham they were free. In fact they were some of the most enslaved people who have ever existed. Israel disobeyed God's laws and under the Assyrian Empire went into slavery in 721 BC. Afterward, these Jews experienced very little liberty for 700 years. Yet they thought and said they were free. Did they have freedom or was it deception?

In His answer to the Jews, Jesus said "freedom" is not connected to Abraham or any man or anything racial or genetic. It is connected to truth. John 8:32 says, "...and the truth shall make you free." It is connected to Christ: "If the Son therefore shall make you free, ye shall be free indeed."

Let us not be too hard on those Jewish people. Today here in America there are millions who have what they think is apparent freedom. But in fact in one way or another they are in bondage. They do not see themselves in slavery, but they are slaves and their bondage severe. The chains of sin can be very tight. A man can let a habit get such a grip on him that he cannot break it. He can allow a pleasure to master him so completely that he cannot do without it. He can let some self-indulgence so dominate him that he is powerless to break away from it. He has no knowledge of the bondage that comes from a desire to be conformed to lifestyles of this world. If you suggest that he is in bondage, he becomes hostile and resentful. "I am doing what I want to do, and I am enjoying my freedom," is his response. Is this freedom or deception?

Perhaps there are many church people who do not fully understand this freedom. The freedom Christ has promised is not a freedom given over to personal indulgence— "do as you please." It is not a freedom from pain and suffering and sorrow. It is not a freedom from temptations and trials. It is not a freedom from making mistakes.

What then is this freedom Christ has provided for us? From various Scriptures I would like for us to explore this important subject. What kind of freedom did Christ promise?

The subject for this July 4 message is this: the freedom Christ brings. John 8:36: "If the Son therefore shall make you free, ye shall be free indeed."

There are three simple truths we should understand about this freedom. I am thinking about the *character* of this freedom, the *cost* of this freedom and the *conditions* for obtaining this freedom.

I. First of all, consider the *character* of this freedom.

What are some of the characteristics of this freedom? There is a freedom you can have from...

...the *corruption* of sin. "...They themselves are the servants of corruption..." (II Peter 2:19). You were redeemed "...with the precious blood of Christ..." (I Peter 1:19).

...the *condemnation* of sin. "There is therefore now no condemnation to them which are in Christ Jesus..." (Romans 8:1).

...the *consequences* of sin. "For the wages of sin is death; but the gift of God is eternal life through Jesus Christ our Lord" (Romans 6:23).

For this message, I would like to spend some extra time focusing on another characteristic.

There is the freedom from the *chains* of sin.

The Bible teaches us that sin has a power, a force, a grip that can be binding and fettering. Listen to the Word of God. "...Whosoever committeth sin is the servant of sin" (John 8:34). Or as it reads in the Amplified version, "...I assure you, most solemnly I tell you, Whoever commits and practices sin is the slave of sin."

Of all the bondage that exists in the world, there is none more horrible than the bondage of sin. Sin and Satan can have such a power over our bodies, our minds and wills that it can become a master (or should I say) a monster. It can dominate, control, your whole being. There is no slavery like the slavery of sin.

But as we have mentioned, most people do not see their actions as sinful. "What's wrong with a little gambling?" "What's wrong with abortion and gay marriage?" "What's wrong in following the fashions of this pagan culture?"

But these are practices that are wrong, sinful. And what is terrifying, some sinful activities can be habit forming. I am thinking especially of those who are hooked on pornography and drugs. There are chains of lust and evil desires. With some the drink habit and the smoke habit have also been binding fetters—and they cannot stop.

I have been a part of many funerals, but perhaps the saddest took place in January 1997. I stood by the casket of a young father, forty-two years of age, leaving behind, weeping and crying, two sons, ages twelve and fourteen, and a sobbing mother. Just a few months previous this young father stood tall and strong and appeared to be in the apex of strength and health. He developed lung cancer. Did his years of smoking have anything to do with this? I will let you answer that question.

In thinking about the freedom that Christ gave, I cannot help but think of….

II. The *cost* in providing this freedom.

As we celebrate our nation's birthday and think about our national freedom, we cannot overlook the cost involved. There was a price paid. We pause to remember those battles and those leaders who fought for our freedom. This was not only true with our founding fathers — across the years for our country's protection, there were many others who risked their fortunes, their families, their reputations, and their lives. We enjoy the freedom we have today because of the price they paid. Freedom is not free.

But I am thinking of another cost. I am thinking of the cost of the freedom the Christian enjoys. Keep in mind this freedom did not come automatically. It did not come by happenstance. It did not come by "silver or gold."

The cost involved — the precious blood of Christ. "Forasmuch as ye know that ye were not redeemed with corruptible things…but with the precious blood of Christ, as of a lamb without blemish and without spot" (1 Peter 1:18, 19).

Ordinarily, the death of anyone is not thought of as "good news." Yet the death of Jesus Christ was good news. I am thinking of the provision made to set us free from the problem of sin in our lives. (II Corinthians 5:21) He died to set us free. We do not have to be slave to sin.

No, we are not overlooking the awful agony Christ suffered. Our hearts are torn when we see Him being nailed to a cross. It was not an easy, gentle passing from this world. It was excruciating agony and torture of the worst kind. It was agony that was…

…*relational*—His friends left Him.

…*abnormal*—He experienced all the pain, all the loneliness, all the torments that have ever been associated with death.

…*physical*—Think of the physical aspects of his death.

He is being nailed to a cross. Do you hear something lashing? It is the sound of a steel whip lashing into the flesh of Jesus. Do you hear water dripping? No, it is not water—it is His blood dripping from His body, dripping on the cold gray rocks of Golgotha. His brow was pierced with thorns. He drank the bitter cup of sorrow to its fullness. I am talking about the provision made for our freedom. His death paints a clear picture of the price paid for our freedom.

I want to close with this final point. Where can this freedom be found? How do we get this freedom? Not only the *character* and *cost* of this freedom, but observe now…

III. The *conditions* in obtaining this freedom.

The freedom Christ brings is freedom from sin. But the question remains to be asked, how do we go about getting this freedom? This freedom does not come automatically. It does not come by happenstance. It is not a product of human effort. There are certain key conditions involved.

A. There is the element of *concern*.

The first step in the pathway to obtaining spiritual freedom starts with an *awareness* of need. We are beginning to see our lost condition. We are not living according to the Bible. I am not a Christian. I am not living as I am supposed to be living. We do not feel comfortable the way we are living. There is a growing concern about our condition. Before someone can repent from sin, he must first realize he is a sinner. We will never seek His grace until we see our need of grace. "For all have sinned, and come short of the glory of God" (Romans 3:23).

B. There is the element of *conviction*.

This awareness of need is sometimes called *conviction*. In order to experience freedom from sin, there is the element of conviction. Conviction of sin is the work of the Holy Spirit which enables us to see our need in true light. We are not always able to see ourselves as God sees us. We are often blind to our failures and our weaknesses. It is the work of the Holy Spirit to show us our true condition. If we are to experience freedom from sin, there must be a full acceptance of the Spirit's work in our lives. We cannot say no to the Holy Spirit and expect freedom. Conviction can be stifled. "And grieve not the holy Spirit of God, whereby ye are sealed unto the day of redemption" (Ephesians 4:30). We thank God for the convicting work of the Holy Spirit.

C. There is the element of *confession*.

Acknowledgement of failure brings up the subject of confession. It is not enough to become aware of one's need. We must confess our need. Conviction, if not stifled and resisted, will result in a spirit of contrition and confession. Acknowledgment of failure is another experience not easily done, but it is all part of the pathway to spiritual freedom. "If we confess our sins, he is faithful and just to forgive us our sins, and to cleanse us from all unrighteousness" (1 John 1:9).

By the way, that little word *if* conveys to us very clearly that there is a condition attached to this freedom. The implication is this—if the Son does not make you free, then there is no freedom. There is nothing but bondage. To find help, we must admit our need.

D. There is the element of *contrition*.

Repentance is the main word we use involving the necessary step toward salvation. But for this message in describing the nature of repentance, I am using the word *contrition*. Contrition is "grieving about and being sorry for one's sins; agonizing guilt." Essentially, it is the feelings of our heart that often follows a period of self-examination. It is a condition which is often misunderstood. True contrition is the necessary prerequisite before God's forgiveness can be received.

John Wesley, the founder of the Methodist revival movement, had an extraordinary insight on this point when he said, "The sinner comes unto the Father with a contrite heart not because he fears the fires of hell, but because he desires forgiveness. The weight of his sin hath bowed his head; the sorrow of his heart hath opened his soul; he is ready now for the forgiveness of God." 2 Corinthians 7:10 says, "…Godly sorrow worketh repentance…"

E. Lastly, there is the commitment of *trust*.

In short the ultimate step in the pathway of obtaining of spiritual freedom lies in one's commitment of trust. "…Believe on the Lord Jesus Christ, and thou shalt be saved…" (Acts 16:31). There is what we call "saving faith."

There are four essential elements or ingredients in saving faith.
1. Saving faith is a yielding to the authority of God, a submitting of myself to His rule.
2. Saving faith is a genuine coming to Christ. We come to Him and cast ourselves upon Him, leaving all other hopes and helps behind.

3. Saving faith consists of the complete surrender of my whole being and life to the lordship of Jesus Christ.
4. Saving faith is a believing on Christ with the understanding, the affections, and the will—that is, with the whole man. All of this is included in true saving faith.

In our commitment to following Christ, we have been set free from the bondage of sin.

In closing, yes, the Fourth of July is a good time to think about freedom. I know the Fourth of July is a day of parades, political speeches, fireworks, and backyard barbecues. I know the Fourth is a good time for travel. This is peak season for vacations, and of course many will be attending religious conferences and camps. Yes, thank God for our national freedom. But there is another kind of freedom. We thank God for the freedom Christ brings—the greatest freedom in all the world.

I close with this poem.

Jesus on the 4th of July
We gather 'round to celebrate
On Independence Day
Pay homage to our country
As the children run and play.

With barbecues and picnics
And fireworks in the air
The flag we own is proudly flown
To show how much we care.

The stars and stripes spell freedom
She waves upon the breeze
While bursts of colors can be seen
Above the towering trees.

This is all quite wonderful
We revel in delight
But God above in divine love
Has brought this day to light.

With just a stroke of liberty
A touch of His great hand
He gave democracy to us
And helped this country stand.

The stripes upon our stately flag
Were touched by His sweet grace
Each star of white that shines so bright
Reflects His loving face.

So as you turn to face the flag
For battles that were fought
Be filled with pride for those who died
And freedoms that were bought.

But don't forget to thank the One
That gives the bright display
The reason why we paint the sky
On Independence Day.

—Marilyn Ferguson

National Adoption Day

10
DIVINE ADOPTION
Romans 8:15, Romans 9:4, Ephesians 1:5, Galatians 4:5

OUR CHURCH CALENDAR holds a number of special days: Mother's Day, Easter, Christmas, Thanksgiving, and on goes the list. But there is one special day which does not attract too much attention. You probably will not find this day listed on any secular calendar. In fact you may not find this day listed on a Christian calendar—it is National Adoption Day.

National Adoption Day is a collective national effort to raise awareness of thousands of orphans and children in foster homes who need to be brought into permanent loving families. Another reason for setting aside this Sunday as a special occasion in our church is to express appreciation to all our parents who have reached out to these needy children. We thank the Lord for these caring couples.

As a pastor, for a long time I felt the need of saying something helpful on the subject of adoption. My first impulse toward developing this message started back in the 1980s. At times hurting couples would pour out their hearts to me. In tears they would say, "Pastor, we can never have children biologically." Their pain was heightened by their involvement with bus ministry children, some of whom were unwanted and uncared for. Infertility is difficult to bear. As pastor I shared with them the need for and importance of adoption.

In the past thirty-five years, adoption has been transformed from a shameful family secret to a praiseworthy act. Because of the rising infertility rates, adoptions have soared. Today in the United States over 22 million people are involved in the adoption process. In one way or another six in ten Americans have had personal experience with adoption. Our state of Florida comes in fourth with the highest number of adoptions.

There is a growing interest in adopting children from the standpoint of ministry—of caring for homeless children. Until recent government restrictions, there has also been a widespread interest in adopting children from other countries. And this has become not only a very common and wonderful practice, but a life-changing ministry.

We have been focusing on the importance of human adoption, and we thank God for this ministry. But now I want to call your attention to another type of adoption. There is spiritual or divine adoption. Adoption is a biblical term expressing one important aspect of initial salvation. Adoption is a beautiful word picture of what God does for us when we come to Christ in faith. We become a child of God.

While the nature of this adoption is entirely different than human adoption, interestingly enough there are various points of similarity between the two. Let us look at these two forms of adoption: natural adoption and divine adoption. Drawing from this parallel, what can we learn from the meaning of these terms? What are some of the experiences involved which appear to be similar?

I. In both adoptions there are
legal implications.

Adoption signifies the act of receiving a stranger into a family and conveying to him legally all the rights, privileges and benefits that belong to a biological child. In human adoption legal steps have to be taken. You do not just go to an orphanage and pick up a child and say, "Hey, you are mine." There is a process involved, and this legal process can be costly. There is a lot of emotion involved in human adoption, but adoption is more than an emotional transaction. It is a legal transaction.

In the placement of a child, the prospective parents must go before a judge. There is questioning. There are documents to be signed and stamped. There is a commitment involved. There is the pounding of the gavel. There is a cost involved. I say again—adoption involves a legal procedure. It is no trivial matter.

Our daughter Evangeline and her husband Rodney were one of those couples who did not want a childless home. Eventually, word came to them that a little brother and sister, ages five and three, had become available for adoption.

After months of legal work, of home visits and anxious waiting, the decision was to be made on a designated day. On the afternoon of June 20, 1989, Vangie called our home. Her first two words were, "Hi, Grandma."

The answer had come. We knew that Jeffrey and Crystal were going to be a part of their home and our family. Their lives and ours would be forever changed. What joy had come to sad, lonely hearts.

After almost a year had past, none of our family will ever forget that special day when we sat in that courtroom and watched the judge pick up his gavel. As he pounded the gavel, he declared that Crystal and Jeffrey were to be the children of Rodney and Evangeline Addison forever. Great joy had come to the Addison home!

Two little children became part of a loving family. That day in May of 1990 two little children received…
…a new last name.
…a new identity.
…a new dad and mom.
…a new grandma and a new grandpa whose lives would also be forever changed.

In divine adoption we know nothing about such legal procedures like you find in human adoption. We are tempted to say, "There is no similarity." There is, however, this one exception. When you surrender your life to Christ, you are brought before the court of heaven. The record of your sinful past becomes blotted out, and you become justified. Your record is clear before God. A judicial declaration has been made: "Son, daughter, you are a child of Mine. You now belong to Me." You are no longer a stranger, an outcast. You are now a part of the family of God. (Galatians 4:7, Ephesians 2:19)

Allow this extra note. Just being religious does not make you a child of God. Joining a church or being born into a Christian family does not make you a child of God. When an individual comes to Christ for salvation, he or she stands before the heavenly tribunal. In this sense, there is a legal aspect involved in our salvation. The heavenly judge erases all traces of the former life, and we are granted a brand new life as a child of God.

In both types of adoption, there are not only *legal implications…*

II. There are *relational implications.*

In human adoption there are changes in relationships. Your relationship to all former connections are severed. New and special relationships are developed. The child takes on a new family name. The adopted child has new parents, new friends, maybe some new brothers and sisters.

Likewise, something like this also happens in spiritual adoption. For one thing, for the believer heavenly relationships are established.

When we are adopted spiritually,

A. We have a new *father*.
"Our Father which art in heaven, Hallowed by thy name" (Matthew 6:9).

B. We gain an *elder brother*.
Being joint-heirs with Christ makes Jesus our Brother. Jesus referred to His disciples as His brothers. "For whosoever shall do the will of my Father which is in heaven, the same is my brother..." (Matthew 12:50).

C. We become related to a *new family*.
New family friendships take place. We not only have a new Father and a new Brother, as an adopted son we now belong to the redeemed family of God. This relationship starts when one becomes saved, and it becomes eternal in that heavenly world. And by the way, we can sing...

> I belong to the King; I'm a child of His love.
> I shall dwell in His palace so fair,
> For He tells of its bliss in yon heaven above,
> And His children in splendor shall share.
>
> I belong to the King, and He loves me I know,
> For His mercy and kindness so free
> Are unceasingly mine wheresoever I go,
> And my Refuge unfailing is He.
>
> *Refrain*
> I belong to the King; I'm a child of His love,
> And he never forsaketh His own.
> He will call me someday to His palace above;
> I shall dwell by His glorified throne.

In both adoptions there are not only *legal implications* and *relational implications*...

III. There are *caring implications*.

There are a number of caring experiences involved in adoption.

A. Adoption is a demonstration of love.

In human adoption, out of love the child is sought after and taken into the family. The child is not sought after because of money. The child is not pursued because the adopting parents have nothing else to do. Adopting couples are not forced to take the child into their home. They do it because they want to pour out their love for the needy child. They want to tell the child, "You are ours. This is your home. We love you."

I saw a cartoon some time ago. Two little brothers were sitting on a bench. One was adopted, the other was a birth child. The adopted boy said to his brother, "Mom and Dad chose me, but they had to take you." I like that.

Dr. Criswell used to tell a remarkable story. Some years ago, a ragged little newsboy was walking down a street. He was an orphan. His paper route took him to some of the more affluent sections of the city. Again and again he passed by elegant, beautiful houses. One day he decided to stop by a beautiful mansion. The lawn was neatly landscaped. The house was expensive and impressive. The driveway was so inviting.

The little lad wandered up the driveway onto the porch. Before he fully realized what he was doing, he rang the doorbell. Mr. Lowry, the owner of the spacious home, opened the door and looked down at the frightened little boy.

Not knowing what to say, the ragged newsboy blurted out, "Mister, do you have a little boy?"

Mr. Lowry, most amused, answered kindly, "No, son, Mrs. Lowry and I don't have any children."

The youngster replied, "Oh, I would give everything I had if I could be your little boy and run and play on this beautiful lawn where nobody could drive me away."

Then in one of those unusual providences of life, Mr. Lowry turned and called upstairs for his wife. The queenly wife walked down that beautiful staircase. Mr. Lowry asked, "Dear, would you like to have a little boy?"

She quickly replied, "Oh, yes!"

And the man turned to the lad and said, "Son, come in. Come right on in."

As the little boy walked into that palatial home, the first thing he did was try to keep his promise. He reached into his pocket, pulled out thirteen cents and offered the pennies to the man. "Sir, this is all I have."

The man took the little boy's hand and closed it around the pennies. He said, "Son, you keep them. I don't need your thirteen cents." He took the lad into his home and heart and adopted him as his son. It was love that made this possible!

This is true in spiritual adoption. There is the element of caring and love. When we came to Christ knocking on the door of salvation, we had nothing to offer—not even thirteen cents. But out of His love, our heavenly Father took us in and adopted us as His child.

It is interesting to see the number of times this concept of love is mentioned in the Scriptures. We cannot underestimate the importance of Divine Love.

"Behold, what manner of love the Father hath bestowed upon us, that we should be called the sons of God…" (I John 3:1).

"'…and I will receive you, and will be a Father unto you, and ye shall be my sons and daughters,' saith the Lord Almighty" (II Corinthians 6:17,18).

"For God so loved the world, that He gave His only begotten son…" (John 3:16).

Spiritual adoption is a living demonstration of God's love. This gospel hymn expresses it so well: "The love of God is greater far than tongue or pen can ever tell. It goes beyond the highest star and reaches to the lowest hell."

The adopted child has the feeling that he has parents who care for him. He can come to them with his needs, and he has no fear of being rejected.

In adoption there is not only an experience of love, but along the same line…

B. Adoption brings the feeling of belonging.

In human adoption the adopted child not only has the assurance of belonging, but the adopted one has all the rights and privileges that a biological child would have. (Galatians 3:7) The possessions of the father belong to his children. The family inheritance will be divided equally among the children.

When my daughter Evangeline and her husband Rodney first brought their soon-to-be adopted children into their home, they showed six-year-old Crystal to her room. She touched the bed and asked, "Is this mine?"

Then she touched the dresser and said, "Is this mine?" And she continued to touch other furniture in the room, asking, "Is this mine?"

Most of her brief life Crystal had lived in foster homes. She never had had her own room and could not believe that all these wonderful things would be actually hers.

With joy Rod and Vangie told Crystal this was her room, her furniture. She was now part of the family. There was a feeling of belonging!

In divine adoption is this not a picture of what happens spiritually? There is a wonderful feeling of belonging.

1. When we belong to God, we can approach God our

Father any time. We can come boldly to the throne of grace. (Hebrews 4:16) The door is always open.
2. When we belong to God, He knows our needs. He gives us His promises. He assures us of His presence. He is concerned about our future.
3. When we belong to God as a part of our divine family, the blessings and benefits that our heavenly Father gives us are amazing. It is more than having a room of your own or anything material. I am now thinking about the promised inheritance that belongs to the adopted child of God. This is how the Apostle Peter states it, "...To an inheritance incorruptible, and undefiled, and that fadeth not away, reserved in heaven for you" (I Peter 1:4).

What a promise! What an inheritance! This beats anything you will ever gain in this life. Material inheritance we eventually have to leave behind. You cannot take one dollar with you. But the children of God have an inheritance that is incorruptible, undefiled, reserved in heaven.

Let me give you a description of this inheritance.

It is an inheritance that is incorruptible. (I Peter 1:4)

It is an inheritance that is eternal.

It is an inheritance that is glorious. "For I reckon that the sufferings of this present time are not worthy to be compared with the glory which shall be revealed in us" (Romans 8:18).

In adoption there is not only an experience of love and a feeling of belonging again, along the same line...

C. Adoption brings a feeling of acceptance.

In natural adoption, in most cases the adopted child not only has the assurance of belonging, he has the feeling of acceptance, He feels wanted. He has parents who care for him. He has no fear of being rejected

During the first few months after Crystal and Jeffery had come to live with my daughter Vangie and Rodney, occasionally Jeffrey would say to my daughter, "If I do something bad, will you give me away?"

Vangie would say, "Oh, no, Jeff, I will never give you away. You are my little son." But, somehow, it really did not seem to register.

Finally, the final proceedings of the adoption morning were completed. The children along with the judge were allowed to pound the gavel. We have precious pictures of that momentous occasion. What a happy day! As a family we went out to eat in a lovely restaurant to celebrate.

Following the meal, we returned to Rod and Vangie's home where Rodney talked to the children and tried to tell them that Jesus had brought them into their lives. Then Grandpa prayed for them. Then Crystal and Jeff went out into the family room to play with their toys. This was in May when we were in the process of leaving the pastorate at Fort Scott and were preparing to move to Hobe Sound to assume the pastorate there.

Leila had brought up a box of some of her games and teaching materials which she had had for some time thinking the children could play with them. In that box was a little hammer that had belonged to Vangie and Paula's pegboard as children.

Jeff spied that little gavel. With the events of the morning apparently still on his mind, he came into the living room and sat down in the middle of the floor. He began to pound the carpet with his little gavel. We could hear him saying something, and we tried to catch what he was saying.

This time he was not saying, "Will you give me away?" No, he was saying, "Your son forever; your son forever." He seemed to understand that now he belonged to the Addisons. A wonderful feeling of belonging.

Thank God for this experience of acceptance. Thank God for the assurance of belonging.

As wonderful as human adoption may be, spiritual

adoption is far greater. What a wonderful thing to belong to the family of God and to enjoy the many benefits and blessings that come to us in our adopted life. And think of those blessings in the world to come. Thank God for this wonderful experience of spiritual adoption.

Once again, a gospel song writer has so poetically depicted this adopted relationship:

> I once was an outcast stranger on earth,
> A sinner by choice, an alien by birth!
> But I've been adopted; my name's written down;
> I'm heir to a mansion, a robe, and a crown.

Let us not overlook this special Sunday—Adoption Sunday. Thank God for the experience of adoption!

Thanksgiving

11
THE GRACE OF GRATITUDE
Colossians 3:15 "...And be ye thankful."

ACCORDING TO A MEDIEVAL legend, two angels were once sent down to earth. One was sent to gather up all the petitions of praying men and women, and the other to collect all the thanksgivings of men and women.

The first angel found petitions everywhere he went. When he returned to heaven, he came with a heavy load on his back filled with petitions and bundles of petitions in each hand. Loaded! The second angel had no such easy time with his assignment. He had to search diligently and patiently for thanksgivings. Finally after a great length of time, he went back to heaven and took with him a mere handful of thanksgivings,

Now legends of course can be farfetched or they can be very near the truth. I have a fear that so many come short in demonstrating this virtue. We are long on our demands, yes, even on our complaints. But we are too short on our thanksgivings—especially those that come from the heart.

I am sorry the second angel did not meet up with me.

If I could, I would have loved to help him fill his wagon to overflowing with thanksgiving. Thanksgiving is one of my favorite times of the year. I love Thanksgiving. By the way, in Christian living it is amazing the attention and emphasis the Apostle Paul gives to this matter of having a thankful spirit. Listen to the music of gratitude that plays thru this epistle alone.

    1: 3 — "We give *thanks* to God and the Father of our Lord Jesus Christ...."

    1: 12 — "Giving *thanks* unto the Father...."

    2: 7 — "...Abounding...with *thanksgiving*."

    3:15 — "...And be ye *thankful*."

    3:17 — "...Giving *thanks* to God and the Father by him."

    4:2 — "Continue in prayer, and watch in the same with *thanksgiving*."

On this Thanksgiving Sunday, I want us to examine this golden virtue of thankfulness the apostle talks about and beautifully demonstrates in his life. In today's world of ingratitude, there cannot be a more important subject.

Research has shown that one of the greatest contributing factors to overall happiness in life is how much gratitude you show. With the help of the Lord, we are ready to accept the challenge of dealing with this important subject *The Grace of Gratitude*.

Before I share my outline of this truth, a basic definition of this word *gratitude* might be very important. What do we mean by the term *gratitude*? Gratitude is the quality of being thankful; readiness to show appreciation and kindness, tenderness of feeling. True gratitude is a grace, or gift from God which proceeds from a humble and transformed heart. In such a case we do not render thanks merely because it is polite or expected or something nice to do. Our actions naturally flow from a profound experience of gratitude. For a child of God, thankfulness is not confined to a day or a season — it is an attitude we should have every day and every hour.

In the development of this needed truth for this Thanksgiving message, I would like to focus our attention involving two areas of concern. I am using a very simple outline: the reasons for gratitude, the results from gratitude. I now would like to share what I think are some of the most important reasons why we need a gratitude practice.

And now for our first lesson.

I. Our *reasons* for gratitude

Expressions of gratitude may be uncommon in some places, but it is not undesirable, and it is surely not unreasonable. What reasons do we have for the practice of gratitude?

For one thing, I am thinking of the many blessings we receive in life—causes for thankfulness. What are some of these blessings? I like the way the hymn writer put it.

With numberless blessings each moment He
   crowns;
And, filled with His fullness divine,
I sing in my rapture, "Oh, glory to God
For such a Redeemer as mine!"

I find joy in making a list of some of these numberless blessings.

A. First on the list above everything else, we are grateful for our *spiritual blessings.*

What are those blessings we enjoy that come from God? Where would we start? What did He give us?

Paul in the Colossians letter tells us of a number of things God has done for us, things for which to be thankful. Let us look at them. Turn to Colossians chapter one, verses twelve through fourteen.

1. (verse 12) He has made us *partakers* of His inheritance.

He has made us fit to share in all the blessings the children of light will enjoy. I thank God for the inheritance incorruptible, undefiled, one reserved in heaven for me. (I Peter 1:4) I thank God for the prospect of our heavenly destiny. Friends, "the toils of the road will seem nothing, when (we) get to the end of the way" (Charles Tillman).

2. (verse 13) He has *delivered* us from the power of darkness.

He has rescued us from the tyranny of sin and transformed us into the kingdom of His dear Son. Marvelous change! Out of darkness into light. Out of defeat into victory.

3. (verse 14) He has *redeemed* us through His blood.

Man, just think what God has done for us! Just think what God has bestowed upon us. Just think who we were before God saved us. We were sinners—lost. Condemned. But, thank God, He paid the ransom to forgive us of our sins and to set us free.

Friends, it is a wonderful thing to know your sins are forgiven. And there is nothing between your soul and the Savior. This is what grace does! Oh, the blessings of grace. Ephesians 2:8: "For by grace are ye saved through faith; and that not of yourselves: it is the gift of God." "Thanks be to God for His unspeakable gift" (II Corinthians 9:15).

In our reasons for gratitude, we have been describing our spiritual blessings. What is next?

B. I am thinking now about our *physical blessings.*

If you have been blessed with good health, you should be most grateful. A grateful spirit promotes a sense of positive wellbeing. Studies suggest gratitude helps to lower blood pressure, strengthen the immune system, reduce symptoms of illness, and make us less bothered by aches and pains. Thanksgiving helps to counteract the poison emitting from nervous needless anxieties. The wise man said, "A merry heart doeth good like a medicine; but a broken (bad) spirit drieth the bones" (Proverbs 17:22).

I am thinking now of personal sickness. Now it is true many people suffer from poor health, and various forms of sickness may take place. While God may allow physical setbacks, He never leaves one without sustaining grace. God never leaves us alone.

Personal note: I am grateful to the Lord for the good health He granted me. For over sixty years as pastor and evangelist, not once did I have to leave my ministry because of poor health. Yes, there were those occasional discomforting physical lumps and bumps, but nothing serious.

C. I am thinking now about our *material blessings*.

Along with the spiritual and physical blessings—while this may not be at the top of the list, we should be grateful as well for the material blessings of life. We who live in the United States have been blessed with material blessing beyond measure.

I am thinking of the nice homes we live in, the modern conveniences we enjoy. I have not forgotten how we lived a few years ago: no microwaves, no automatic dishwashers, no cell phones, no air-conditioning, no computers, no modern stoves—wow!

The car I now drive is somewhat different from the '52 Ford I once owned. I now can attend church in my own home—internet. The "out-houses" are about gone. I appreciate the modern showers in our bathrooms. Enough said!

Again, while these may not be the main reasons for showing a spirit of thankfulness, it would not hurt once in a while to stop and think about how much God has helped in giving us guidance in where we should live, what we should buy, what investments we should make.

Yes, thank God for our material blessings.

Having listed various reasons for the practice of gratitude, observe now...

II. The *results* of gratitude

What would be some of the results of gratitude?

A. Gratitude pleases the Lord.

Christ is not mindless of a grateful heart and a thankful spirit. Psalm 92:1: "It is a good thing to give thanks unto the Lord, and to sing praises unto thy name, O Most High." Psalm 103:2: "Bless the Lord, O my soul, and forget not all his benefits."

The story of the ten lepers is a good illustration of this truth. The Master was pleased when the healed leper came back to thank the Lord for his healing. In effect the Master was saying, "I appreciate you coming back and thanking me for your healing, but where are the nine?" Christ is never mindless when we seek to praise Him for the benefits of His love and grace. He is pleased when He sees a grateful heart in His children.

B. Gratitude brings adornment to our life.

Have you ever stopped to think what makes a person beautiful and attractive? It takes more than powder and paint to make a person attractive. It takes more than Walmart jewelry to adorn the body. Nothing so beautifies the life as a thankful spirit.

The kind of jewelry you need to wear are the jewels of kindness, meekness and humbleness. If you have a beautiful spirit and a thankful attitude, people will appreciate you and enjoy being around you. No one enjoys being around a grumbler.

Nothing can adorn the spirit of man more becomingly than genuine thankfulness in all the circumstances of life.

C. Gratitude often improves, strengthens our relationships with others.

Gratitude is also a powerful tool for strengthening interpersonal relationships. People who express their gratitude tend to be more willing to forgive others. Whether it is a friend, colleague, family member or acquaintance, we all have someone in our lives who has been a positive influence. Taking a moment to tell them—whether in person or through a letter, email, text or phone call—will not only make them feel better, but it will benefit you, too. It can also help improve the quality of your relationships. Try telling your spouse or children why you are grateful for them. You will be amazed at the positive influence it can have on the relationship.

D. Gratitude often helps protect you from toxic, negative emotions such as envy, resentment, regret—emotions that can destroy our happiness.

You cannot feel resentful and grateful at the same time. They are incompatible feelings. People who have high levels of gratitude have low levels of resentment and envy. For one thing if you are grateful, you cannot resent someone for having something you do not have. Gratitude blocks emotions that can destroy happiness.

In the development of the grace of gratitude, I would like to share two final results.

E. The grace of gratitude fulfills biblical expectations.

One result of being thankful is the feeling that you are being biblical in your living. I do not know how many times the Word of God exhorts us to be thankful. It is a requirement! In one letter alone the Apostle Paul exhorts thankful living over half a dozen times. The apostle does not locate this business of gratitude among the luxuries of the Christian life. He gives it a place among the necessities.

So it might seem a bit strange that we need to be reminded that we should give thanks. But experience bears out the fact that too many times we take the blessings of life, the blessings of God as a matter of course. Gratitude has become a very scarce commodity in these modem times. In fact Saint Paul notes that one of the characteristics of the people in the last days is this matter of being unthankful. (II Timothy 3:2)

F. The grace of gratitude can be a rewarding practice.

You never lose when there is a display of kindness, thoughtfulness and tenderness. This is so true in family relationships. In the home think of the results that criticism and faultfinding can have. There was an event that happened in my first pastorate I will never forget. My neighbor friend attended our church faithfully, but his son would never come. I tried faithfully to get Don to come. One day I found out why. On one occasion I was in the kitchen of his house doing some work. In the living room I heard the father constantly criticizing a number of members of his church. I got my answer why the son would not come. Thank God, in my sixty years of ministry this was a rare occasion. This kind of stuff does not happen where kindness, charitableness, goodness exists.

By the way, I am thankful for my wonderful family They are my favorite people. What a blessing it is to have a Christian family committed to Christian ministries. A little humor—I am so thankful for a wonderful wife. She has put up with me now for over sixty years. Grace is rewarding!

This is the Sunday of Thanksgiving week. Have a great Thanksgiving Day, and be thankful to God for all your blessings!

CHRISTMAS SUNDAY

12
WISE MEN STILL SEEK CHRIST
Matthew 2:1-2

A NUMBER OF YEARS AGO, a boy came running home after a Sunday morning service and called, "Mommy, Mommy, I've got a part in the Christmas play."

His mother replied, "What part do you have, Tom?"

"I'm one of the three wise guys!"

This little bit of humor brings back some memories of my first church and my first experience in preparing a Christmas program. We had some boys who came only to Sunday School. They were not a part of the church. I wanted to get them involved, so I made them wise men. But I made a mistake. The night of the program outside of the church, my wise men got into a snowball fight, and they would not speak to each other. They never did make it to Bethlehem. These wise men were not too wise.

As a pastor during the month of December, I enjoyed studying those Scriptures which were related to the characters of Christmas. For this message we want to talk about those men who traveled from the East to find Christ. It is interesting to note that Matthew is the only Gospel writer who records the visit of these wise men who traveled to worship the Christ child.

With many of these Gospel stories, sometimes humanly speaking I wish the biblical writers would have given us a little more detail. While we do not question the inspiration of Scripture, on occasion we are left to wonder. My curiosity gets the best of me as I contemplate some of the missing details of the story. I wonder...

Was the Apostle Paul ever married?
Did Noah sleep well during the flood?
Did Peter ever try walking on water again?
I wonder... and the list could go on.

The story of the wise men is no exception. I often wonder who exactly were these wise men? We are not told. What was their country of origin? We are not told, except they came from the East. We might wonder, where did they go after they left Bethlehem?

Our imagination is set on fire with a burning curiosity. There is a sense of mystery here. We are intrigued by these unusual visitors. It would have been nice to have a few more facts provided.

Legend and medieval tradition have a few more answers for us. From legend we know how many wise men there were and how many miles they traveled. We know they were kings. We even know their names. We know they became disciples. In telling the story of the wise men, we must be careful we do not get fiction and fact mixed up. I have a concern that our poets and artists have drawn more on legend than on Scripture.

And yet while little is known, these ancient travelers did leave behind some helpful lessons to guide us in our worship of Christ. I would like to talk about these men who came seeking Christ. Let us focus on what we do know.

Our thoughts are directed around this theme... *wise men still seek Christ.* I would like to center our thoughts around three simple statements:

I. What these wise men sought

"…Where is he that is born King of the Jews? for we have seen his star in the east, and are come to worship Him" (Matthew 2:2).

You know the story. These men had some vacation time on their hands. They wanted to spend that time visiting another country. So they checked with their local travel agency and made arrangements for a Holy Land tour. We cannot criticize this noble aspiration. I have been there a couple times myself.

However, that is not the case here. While there is nothing wrong with a Holy Land visit, these men were not on a vacation nor a sightseeing trip. Their objective was finding Christ. They were on a quest to find Jesus. Listen to their cry, "Sirs, we would see Jesus."

I see two important truths concerning their quest to seek Christ.

A. These men sought Christ as a compelling concern.

No doubt, as working heads of households and perhaps community leaders, I am sure they had plenty of other responsibilities. But this quest to find Christ became the compelling force in their lives. This became their primary concern.

B. Seeking Christ was not a side issue.

If they had access to the Scriptures, no doubt they were familiar with Numbers 24:17: "…There shall come a Star out of Jacob, and a Sceptre shall rise out of Israel.…" Matthew chapter two tells us in verse ten: "When they saw the star, they rejoiced.…" And they started on their search for the newborn king of the Jews.

For years these seekers of truth may have looked with anticipation for a star indicating the Messiah had come. In the study of astronomy, this became the central focus of their interests. There was a compelling search to find Christ.

On occasion, it might not hurt to ask ourselves these questions:
- What is the compelling interest in my life?
- What am I living for?
- What is the supreme quest of my life?

For a lot of people today, their goals in living center around material gain, not spiritual things. They are controlled by material ambitions. The big thing is having a good car, good house, good income, plenty of money. There is nothing wrong in making money. But is that the ultimate goal in living?

In seeking for something to fill the void, the emptiness in life, they find some earthly joys and some measure of happiness. It is interesting to see what people seek after in our culture today. The search is endless. Many today are worshiping the gods of lust, of pleasure, the gods of sensual concerns.

One glance at the headlines of our newspapers should convince you of our nation's mad quest for pleasures. I read just recently that one family spent six hundred dollars on booze for a weekend party on their Palm Beach estate. Booze cannot fill the void of an empty heart. Worldly pleasures cannot satisfy the hunger of the human soul. But the God of heaven can fill that void.

What should be our ultimate goal? The greatest wisdom is to make Jesus the controlling compelling focus of your life. Wise men still seek Christ.

C. In a sense these men sought Christ as a constant, persistent concern.

These men provide inspiring examples of spiritual earnestness and perseverance. They faced all kinds of obstacles. There was a distance factor—it was a long journey. There would be all kinds of weather. King Herod could neither dissuade nor distract them in their quest to find Christ.

They could have easily given up, packed up their duds and gone back home. But they were persistent in their search. They sought Jesus until they found Him.

We face a constant danger of missing God's blessing by allowing various distractions to change our course of action Those who diligently seek after Christ will find Him.

Allow this one extra note. In the case of these wise men seeking Christ, their quest was not a popular one. These men were not affected by the fact that no one else seemed very interested in the celebration of this birth. They did not have to wait in line to get to see Jesus. If crowds were filling the highways leading to Jerusalem, they were not coming to find Jesus. And when the crowds came to Bethlehem, they did not come to see Jesus. They came to pay their taxes.

Interestingly enough, this fact did not affect their decision. These men sought Christ with a persistent personal concern. They did not yield to peer pressure.

To be honest about it, peer pressure has a lot to do with some of our decisions. Most of us do not like to be too different. We want to fit in. We do what the crowd is doing. We need to feel connected.

It is peer pressure that leads youth to reject Biblical values.

It is peer pressure that motivates teens to pick up dangerous habits.

It is peer pressure that sends us off in the wrong direction.

But these men were not affected by peer pressure.

II. What these wise men brought

These men brought gifts to baby Jesus. It is interesting to consider the kind of gifts they brought to this Child and the reason for these gifts. To be honest about it, these were not typical presents you would normally give to a baby. In modern language why did they not go to a shopping mall or thrift store somewhere and buy a stuffed animal or some little hat or some little toy suitable for children? What were the gifts they brought to this Christ-child? "...They presented unto him gifts; gold, and frankincense and myrrh" (Matthew 2:11).

What did these gifts represent?

A. These were *devotional* gifts showing their love for Christ.

So little information is given about the wise men themselves, but their worship gifts are mentioned in detail.

B. These were *appropriate* gifts.

1. Gold — It is easy to see why gold is an appropriate gift for Jesus Christ. Gold is the metal of kings. When gold was presented to Jesus, it acknowledged His right to rule. The wise men knew Jesus was the King of kings.
2. Incense — Incense was also a significant gift. It was used in temple worship. It was mixed with the oil that was used to anoint the priests of Israel. It was part of the meal offerings that were offerings of thanksgiving and praise to God. In presenting this gift, the wise men pointed to Christ as our great High Priest, the one whose whole life was acceptable and well pleasing to His Father.
3. Myrrh — Myrrh was used for embalming. By any human measure it would be odd — if not offensive — to present to the infant Christ a spice used for embalming. But it was not offensive in this case, nor was it odd. It was a gift of faith. We do not know precisely what the wise men may have known or guessed about Christ's ministry. But we do know the Old Testament again and again foretold His suffering.

What gifts do we offer? Giving our tithe to Christ is important. It can be an indication of our devotion to Jesus. It is a material manifestation of our submission to Him.

But the most important gift we give to Christ is not just our money. It is our life, our love, our loyalty, our obedience. The greatest gift we can give is to give our lives to Him. If He has my heart, He has everything else.

We must have the same attitude that an Indian had who testified, "Indian lay down blanket. Indian lay down pipe. Indian lay down tomahawk. Indian lay down Indian." It is important to give to Him our blanket and tomahawk. But God wants the Indian.

Let us move on. There is one more fact we need to look at. What these wise men *sought*; what these wise men *brought*...

III. What these wise men taught

What can we learn from this fascinating account? What wisdom can we gain from these wise men? From their actions they teach us four things.

A. We learn something about *following divine leadership*.

The wisdom of these wise men centered first in the fact that they followed God's leadings. To their receptive minds the guiding star was the finger of God moving across the heavens, and they followed the star.

Are you sensitive to God's leadings? This truth has not changed from that day to this. The truly wise man is the one who follows the leading of God. These learned men from the East were not given a roadmap to follow. They were simply given a star. They followed the light they had, and God honored them for it.

The writer of Proverbs tells us if we acknowledge God in all our ways, He will direct our path. (Proverbs 3:6) God gave the children of Israel a cloud by day and a pillar of fire by night to follow. He gave the wise men a star to lead them. It is true He does not deal with most of us that dramatically, but He has promised to go before us. If we are willing to take one step—one step—toward the Lord, He will take two steps toward us. Wise men today as always are those who follow divine leadership.

B. We learn something about *faith*.

These wise men were wise because they responded in faith. I am sure their friends must have thought these men were out of their minds. "Where are you going? What are you doing? It doesn't make sense leaving everything behind and following some strange star."

What then do we learn from these wise men? It is wisdom to follow the journey of faith no matter how difficult the road may appear. Many times God wants us to make a journey of faith. He asks us to step out into new areas where we have not gone before. We may not be sure of exactly where we are going, but we go in faith. Am I willing to trust God as much as the wise men did? Heavenly wisdom is always far superior to earthly wisdom.

C. We learn something about *worship*.

"…They saw the young child… and fell down, and worshipped him…" (Matthew 2:11). The wisdom of the wise men was demonstrated in the fact that they worshiped the Christ child. They did not come to show admiration—they came to show devotion.

There are several elements involved in true worship that are pictured for us in this account. We learn that…

1. True worship involves a spirit of *commitment*.

The Magis' commitment to worship is evident in their willingness to risk the safety of their lives to bow at Jesus' feet. This was not a sightseeing trip. There were barriers they had to overcome. But in spite of all the hindrances, nothing stopped them in their commitment to worship. Does not this kind of commitment stand in bold contrast to what we find today among modern churchgoers? Christmas is a time of gift giving, but most importantly it is a special time for worship.

We learn that...

2. True worship involves a spirit of *humility*.

We learn from Scriptures (Matthew 2:11) that the wise men came to the house, they saw the young child, and they fell down and worshiped Him. They bowed before Him. Bowing is a sign of honor that is rooted in an attitude of humility.

What a scene we have before us. Here are some of the wisest men of the world now bending before a little helpless child. Here are men of stature and wealth and rank kneeling before poverty. Here they were on their faces before Jesus.

What were they doing? They were acknowledging that they were in the presence of Someone greater than they were. They felt their unworthiness.

Friends, when we come bowing before Him in true worship, we come confessing our own failures, our own needs, our own littleness. You do not come to God standing up and telling God how great you are and how good you are and how nice you are. You come to God acknowledging your weaknesses, your shortcomings. You come sharing your concerns.

We learn that...

3. True worship involves a spirit of *praise*.

"When they saw the star, they rejoiced with exceeding great joy" (Matthew 2:10). Underline the expression "exceeding great joy." Who can describe the joy these men felt when they saw the star again and knew they would soon see the Christ Child?

Undoubtedly, it is with divine purpose that Matthew included the story of the wise men. From them there are lessons to be learned as we consider what these men *sought*, what they *brought*, and what they *taught*.

The star of hope is still shining. Wise men still seek Him.

13
MARY— QUALITIES TO FOLLOW
Luke 1:26-38

It is incredible to think that another year has slipped by, and we are coming into the heart of the Christmas season. Now I enjoy preaching messages on Christmas. And today we want to start a series of messages dealing with some great themes that emerge from the Christmas story. The themes I am selecting are spoken to us from the lives of those people who make up the Christmas story. Cultures differ, but the human heart is the same. There is a sense that these lives in this Gospel account are no different from us. Do not count them as irrelevant because they belong to a different day. Their reaction to the coming of Christ provides for us powerful teaching values that are contemporary and timeless.

For our first study I would like to place our focus upon Mary, the mother of our Lord. If I were to choose a title it would be this: *Qualities to Follow.*

To be honest, across the many years of ministry I have not given much attention to Mary. To me Mary seemed so much like the nativity figure. After Christmas we put away all the nativity scenes, and we sort of forget Mary. In recent years, however, I have developed a growing appreciation for this mother.

In the Protestant world we may not say enough about Mary. No, we are not to worship Mary. We are not to pray to Mary. She has no ability to answer our prayers. She is not the fourth person of the Trinity. Yet I wonder if there are not some lessons we can learn from her life. Let us not set Mary apart and think of her only at Christmastime. Incidentally, in the Scriptures Mary is mentioned several times beyond the Christmas story. (Matthew 12:46, John 19:25) Years have passed by. The last time we hear of Mary, she is in the Upper Room praying with the disciples, all in one accord. (Acts 1:14)

The Gospel of Matthew and Luke teach us many things about Mary. Her life is worthy of study. For one thing, in looking at these Gospel glimpses afforded us, I am finding that Mary demonstrates character strengths that are exemplary. What can we learn from her life? What are some of those qualities that mark out her life? For one thing…

I. There is the quality of *humility*.

In thinking about the life of Mary, we cannot overlook her spirit of humility. There is an element of humility that runs thru her entire life. I believe one reason she was chosen to be used of God was for the quality of humility seen early in her life. God does not use people who are full of pride, arrogant and self-centered.

Her humility is especially displayed in the Christmas story. As a young girl an angel came to visit Mary. What is so interesting is to look at her reaction when confronted with Angel Gabriel. I am amazed at her response. Here is this humble poor Jewish peasant girl from a small town. She was not a daughter of some rich ruler or some rich scribe. There is no earthly distinction. But here she was being visited by an heavenly angel. Wow! What an honor. To tell you the truth, if I ever had an heavenly angel come to visit me like this, I could not wait to put it on Facebook. I could not wait to tell others. No, this was not the action or attitude of Mary. Mary's response was one of humility.

What was happening? In this visit with the heavenly angel, Mary was told of some supernatural things that were going to happen to her. She was shocked at what the angel was saying. What God wants would change her life forever. As a virgin she was to become pregnant through the miracle-working power of the Holy Spirit. She was to give birth to a son, and His name would be called Jesus.

In verse 34 we read of Mary's response to this messenger. It is what Mary does not say that I find interesting. She does not say, "Gabriel, you've got to be kidding me. This is just unbelievable. Are you being real?"

No, what we do read is this. "Then said Mary unto the angel, How shall this be, seeing I know not a man" (verse 34)? "And Mary said, Behold the handmade of the Lord; be it unto me according to thy word..." (verses 38). In other words this young girl was saying "I don't understand it all—and I am sure others won't understand it either. But I am His servant. Whatever God wants, I want." Among other qualities, her response was one of humility.

Here is a good question to ask: what would you do if you were Mary?

This business of meekness and humility is not the most popular quality in today's living, I do not recall seeing too many books on "How To Be Humble." I do remember some quotes.

> I bet I'm twice as humble as you are.
> He who falls in love with self will have no rivals.
> Conceit is God's gift to little men.

His only fault is that he has no faults.
When you're as great as I am, it's hard to be humble.

Yes, humility may not be very popular, but the fact is humility is the distinguishing mark of the true disciple of Christ. The Scriptures are clear about the kind of heart God blesses.

"Blessed are the meek: for they shall inherit the earth" (Matthew 5:5). "Blessed are the poor in spirit: for theirs is the kingdom of heaven" (Matthew 5:3). God puts tremendous emphasis on humility.

Beyond the Christmas story, in all the accounts we have of Mary—and there are several—we find no record of Mary bragging on herself, saying, "I'm the mother of Jesus." Mary did not exalt herself to more than being a handmaid of the Lord. Her response was one of humility.

In Mary's life we not only see the quality of humility, but...

II. There is the quality of *obedience*.

What makes this Christmas story so important is you cannot look at Mary's life and not learn something about obedience. For one thing we learn that her act of obedience involved an act of submission. The path of submission is not always an easy one to follow.

It is not easy when your heart is set on following your own plans and wishes. And what Mary planned for was important. She was engaged to a wonderful man named Joseph. They were soon to get married. But God's plan for her life was different. Sometimes what God wants cuts right across our human desires and wishes. A struggle exists—my will, God's will.

For a moment look at the difficulty involved in her submitting to God's will. Look at what Mary faced when she said yes to God.

A. I am sure she thought about the risk of family rejection.

What would her parents say? She had to confront Mom and Dad and brothers. What had happened? Here she is with Child and not married. In those days there was a terrible stigma involved. She could lose her life. A young girl pregnant out of wedlock in that culture would be absolutely unbelievable. But you say, "I believe her parents supported her." It may be they did. But I wonder? They probably believed her, just like you would believe your sixteen-year-old daughter, when she came home and said, "Mom, I've got some news for you."

"What's that, daughter?"

"I got pregnant, Mom. It's a miracle. God is going to give me a child without a husband." I would say there would be some long family discussion over that answer.

B. I am sure she encountered the risk of public rejection.

What do you think her friends said? Can you imagine the gossip in that small town? To be found with child and not married. They did not have abortion clinics in those days. Thank God.

C. I am sure she thought about the risk of Joseph's rejection.

When she said yes, she was saying, "I am willing to lose the prospect of Joseph being my husband. Being a careful righteous man, he won't understand." And by the way, she would not only be losing a husband but the lifelong support a husband would bring to her. Her economic future would be lost. Not only would Joseph have nothing to do with her, neither would the other young men who were decent, upstanding.

But what was Mary's response? Yes, she was troubled. Yes, she had some questions about it all. But with a thinking mind, sensitive heart, and a humble spirit, she traveled the path of obedience. She listened to the heavenly voice, and she did it with joy even though she did not understand all that was taking place and how everything would turn out. Mary submitted her life, her future, to God's will.

Look at this verse again. "And Mary said, Behold the handmaid of the Lord (I am your servant; I belong to you, Lord, body and soul.); be it unto me according to thy word (Let it be, Lord, whatever you want.)…" (Luke 1:38).

Friends, what are we saying here? There may be times in our life when God calls us to make a decision that will appear to be crazy to others. They just do not understand.

Do you remember the story of Noah? Noah provides us a classic example. That antediluvian crowd did not understand old Noah. For years Noah faced nothing but ridicule and sneers. He was considered a religious nut. They thought he was crazy. They had never seen any rain! Here he is building a boat. This guy has gone crazy.

What are we saying? There may be times in our life when God calls us to make a decision that will appear to be crazy to others. They just do not understand.

Mark it down—choosing God's way may not always make you popular in our pagan society. Your standards of conduct will not be the same as those of a godless world. Your values will be different. Your lifestyles are different.

In previous years at Hobe Sound Bible College, we had quite a number of students from Taiwan. Some of those students who came to us had made a commitment to serve Christ. But by doing so, it meant rejection from their parents and their friends back home. To turn to Christ, they had turned their back upon all that was dear to them in their past life.

I am thinking of Carol Chuang. Carol was a first-year student at Hobe Sound. She had a Buddhist background, and her parents did not understand our Christian religion. It was fine for her to come to further her education, but she was not to embrace our belief. However, she became a truly born again Christian and felt she needed to be baptized. She requested prayer, but it was a very difficult decision. Her father threatened to drop her support if she continued in college.

After several months Carol decided she needed to be baptized. Her parents begged her not to go through with this. We asked Carol why she felt it was so important to be baptized. She said, "It isn't enough to say I'm a Christian. This is a sign that I belong to Him, and I want the world to know Jesus is my Savior. I want to be an example for Him."

Those who were there on that Easter Sunday will not forget that occasion. Carol's face glowed with God's glory as she came out of the water. She gave a strong testimony of determination to follow Jesus. The Chinese culture is very respectful of their parent's wishes, and Carol was no exception. Her parents loved her dearly, and she wanted to make them happy. The night before her baptism, she called her parents. Her father became so angry he said he never wanted to hear that word again and hung up.

It cost Carol something She was rejected by her parents. She turned her back on all that was dear and near to her to follow Christ. Yes, I hope and pray that someday Carol's parents will change their minds. At any rate, Carol presently enjoys belonging to the family of God, having the support of brothers and sisters she never had before. More than anything else, she enjoys the blessing and presence of God in her life—and that is what really counts. You never lose in submitting your life to Christ.

There is not only the quality of *humility* and *obedience*...

III. There is the quality of *faith*.

In this Christmas account of Mary, there is another quality that is exemplary, a quality that cannot be overlooked. I marvel at the faith Mary displayed. Faith goes hand in hand with obedience.

At the time of her visitation with her cousin, Elizabeth took notice of this, and she praised Mary for her faith. "Blessed are you who believed that what was spoken to you by the Lord would be fulfilled" (Luke 1:45 NABRE).

I do not think those were empty words. I cannot help but ask this question—what did she see in Mary's faith that prompted this testimony? I believe several aspects could be mentioned.

A. I am sure Elisabeth was praising Mary for the faith she had as a teenager.

Talk about miracles! Elisabeth herself was giving birth to a son at seventy years of age. But you do not have to get old to see what faith can do. We learn this lesson—faith is not age-dependent. We are impressed with the mature faith this young girl Mary displayed.

B. Elisabeth was praising Mary in believing God for the impossible.

Mary was asked to do something that had never happened before. I know this story of Mary's faith is most unusual, but it is still true. He is the God who can do the seeming impossible. That is as true today as it was 2,000 years ago.

This is good news for all of us. Some are carrying heavy burdens today. For some of you Christmas will be lonely this year. Some of you are facing a financial crisis that looks hopeless to you right now. Some of you are out of work and do not have a single lead on a good job. Some of you have children who are far away from God. Some of you feel lonely and far away from God yourselves.

The list goes on and on. But all these things have this in common: they seem impossible to solve by any human means. And for the most part they are. After all if human means would have solved your problems, they would have been solved long ago. But God is still on the throne. He is still the God of the impossible.

As the old gospel song puts it: "Got any rivers you think are uncrossable? Got any mountains you cannot tunnel through? God specializes in things thought impossible. He does things that others cannot do."

In closing we have been looking at what God wanted from Mary...

IV. I wonder what God wants from us?

What about these qualities of humility, obedience and faith? Are these strong governing factors in our Christian life? Is there any need for improvement? Can we say with Mary "Lord, whatever you want. Thy will be done." No, we may not know all the "whys and the wherefores." But we can hold steady! We can leave the unknown future in the Master's hands. We can give those tangled mysteries to Jesus. Someday He will show us the reason why. He will tell us all about it. In the meantime we will trust Him and say yes to His will. "Where we can't trace Him, we can trust Him." Remember, we are not seeing the big picture yet.

What is it that God wants from us? Total comprehension about the future before we will trust Him? No, that is impossible. And besides, it is better that we do not know what the future holds. Does He want us to have perfect knowledge of the Bible? The answer is no. Very few of us would meet that qualification. What does God want from us? The same thing He wanted from Mary—simple faith that He will keep His word in unlikely and unexpected ways. "Be it unto me according to thy word."

Our Father, we do not pray for more faith. We pray rather for courage to exercise the faith we already have. Make us more like Mary, willing to believe in spite of our fears. We pray in the name of Him whose birth we celebrate at this time of year. Amen.

14
THE WORLD'S GREATEST GIFT
John 3:16, II Corinthians 9:15

DECEMBER IS THE MONTH when our minds are turned toward giving and receiving gifts. Have you ever thought where all this gift business began? There is a modern trend to do away with the word *Christmas*. The word *holiday* is used in place of Christmas. Be sure to buy your *holiday gifts* today.

But let us be mindful. There is more to Christmas than shopping and Santa Claus. We must never forget the original and wonderful gift that was given to us over 2,000 years ago—the gift that was given by God—the greatest gift this world has ever received.

Before we close this Christmas season, let us turn our thoughts to this gift given. Someone called this little child in Bethlehem's manger the "Indescribable Gift." The Apostle Paul was not toying with words when he called Jesus "God's Unspeakable Gift." (II Corinthians 9:15) For this Christmas sermon, the question I am asking is, "What made this gift so indescribably great?" To answer this delightful question, let us think about how we value gifts. Then let us apply these standards to the gift that was given to us from heaven.

How do you value a gift? Why is one gift more valuable than another? What are the standards we use to determine the value of a gift?

I. A gift may be determined valuable because of the *motive* involved.

What are the motives that prompt people to give?

Gifts can be given out of duty. "If we don't give our neighbor a gift, he would be disappointed." Gifts are often given out of obligation.

Gifts can be given for personal gain. The interest is in self.

Gifts can be given to impress people. We want something in return.

But the gift of Bethlehem was not given for any of these reasons. The nature and motive of this gift was totally different. The gift of this baby was motivated, prompted, by the greatest love ever demonstrated. There was no self-interest.

What does John 3:16 tell us? "For God so loved the world..." The word so is small but powerful. It speaks of the greatness of His love. It was the love of God that moved Him to sacrifice His only Son for sinful mankind. (Romans 5:8)

While His love can never be adequately described, we do thank our song writers for their descriptive efforts.

> The love of God is greater far
> Than tongue or pen can ever tell.
> It goes beyond the highest star
> And reaches to the lowest hell.
> The guilty pair, bowed down with care,
> God gave His Son to win;
> His erring child He reconciled
> And pardoned from his sin.
>
> —Frederick Lehman

Perhaps we should observe a few descriptive notes about this love.

A. It is a *universal* love.

"God so loved *the world*." His love is not racial—it is universal; not local—but global. It was not limited to a certain group or a chosen few. No, His love takes in the entire world.

B. It was a *sacrificial* love.

"God so loved the world *that He gave His only begotten Son.*" This love was so great that it caused God to sacrifice His Son to save a sinner.

C. It was a *redemptive* love.

It was a love so great that it offered pardon for the guilty, purity for the unclean, peace for the troubled heart, help for the sick, comfort for the dying.

Charles Wesley penned these lyrics:
>And can it be that I should gain
>An interest in the Savior's blood
>Died He for me, who caused His pain?
>For me, who Him to death pursued?
>Amazing love! how can it be
>That Thou, my God shouldst die for me?
>Amazing love! how can it be
>That Thou, my God, shouldst die for me.

Across the years the Pierpoint family always deeply appreciated the wonderful Christmas cards sent to the parsonage and especially those extra words of love and appreciation. But the greatest Christmas card ever given to me was given many years ago by my own daughter Evangeline. She was a little girl at that time in first grade. I still have the card. I treasure it. It was handmade. The card really was not very beautiful, nor pretty. The card was made with a little piece of paper somewhat torn and smudged. And on that card were these words, "I LOVE YOU, DADDY. MERRY CHRISTMAS." That card was a projection of her love which made it valuable to me above all other cards.

II. A gift may be determined valuable because of the *uniqueness* involved.

Occasionally, we receive gifts that are totally different. There are individuals who are specialists in giving unique gifts. You can depend on it. The gift will be different.

When I was pastoring in Fort Scott, Kansas, I did a little teaching in their academy. I was in charge of the chapel services and the Bible courses. One Christmas time, some of my students in my Bible class gave me an anonymous Christmas gift. They presented it first to my daughter who was told it was for their teacher. She was instructed to take the box to her father, not revealing who it was from. Likewise, it was not to be left in the cold car.

Paula came home from school. "Daddy, you have a Christmas box in the car. Some of the students bought a Christmas present for you this year." Instantly, something struck me strange. These kids have never done this before. Why is Paula insisting that I bring it inside? Finally, Paula had to go and retrieve the gift.

"Daddy, here is your gift."

I lifted the box. "Oh, Paula, there is something live in this box. I am not opening it."

Finally, Paula had to opened it. And there it was—a hamster! Wow! Certainly this gift was indeed unique, but for me it had no value at all. It was not my cup of tea. The thought of having this "mouse" running around my office chair was more than I could handle. I gave this gift to an animal lover who I thought might enjoy it. Gifts are valuable when they are useful and meet a specific need.

In serious thinking about unique gifts, Christmas is the

celebration of a gift that is most unique. There is much that is not ordinary about the birth of the little baby lying in that manger. Let us enumerate those unusual aspects concerning the birth of Christ.

A. He was born in a stable.

If you were to come to visit this newborn baby, you would not find Him in a palace but a smelly stable. For this baby, there would be no array of silk, sachets and satin—nothing but straw. You would not see earthly royalty. In this stable there is heavenly humility. No celestial choirs or Bethlehem bands would perform here, but only the braying of a donkey, the barking of a dog, the bleating of the sheep.

B. He was a child of promise.

The coming of this little child was announced 4,000 years before He was born. This baby was a subject of biblical prophecy. "Therefore the Lord Himself will give you a sign: Behold, a virgin will be with child and bear a son, and she will call His name Immanuel" (Isaiah 7:14 NASB).

C. His birth was announced by an angel.

The quiet of that Judean night was broken by the voice of an angel appearing in the sky announcing that a baby was born in Bethlehem. "For unto you is born this day in the city of David a Saviour, which is Christ the Lord" (Luke 2:11).

D. He was born without an earthly father.

This infant was conceived by the Holy Spirit. "...The Holy Spirit will come upon you, and the power of the Most High will overshadow you..." (Luke 1:35 NASB).

E. He was a child void of a sinful nature.

Jesus was the sinless Son of God. It was through this child that God stepped down from Heaven and entered frail human flesh. "Who committed no sin, nor was any deceit found in His mouth" (I Peter 2:22 NASB).

F. He was a child who was born to die.

Those soft little hands fashioned by the Holy Spirit in Mary's womb would someday be pierced through with nails. Those baby feet, pink and unable to walk, would one day walk up a dusty hill to be nailed to a cross. That sweet infant's head with sparkling eyes and eager mouth would someday have a crown of thorns forced upon it. "...He Himself bore our sins in His body on the cross, so that we might die to sin and live to righteousness; for by His wounds you were healed" (1 Peter 2:24 NASB). *Jesus was born to die.*

III. A gift may be determined valuable because of the *purpose* involved.

The gift may look attractive and be costly. But if it does not meet a need or serve some purpose for the recipient, it really has little value for him. The item may be found a year later at a garage sale.

At first for the average citizen of Bethlehem there was nothing significant about the birth of this baby born in a barn. The surroundings were rough and rugged, inferior and inadequate. But lo, a brilliant star announced this birth. Prophets proclaimed His forthcoming. There is a purpose for this Babe in Bethlehem's manger. Jesus was born to become our Savior. He came "to seek and to save that which was lost" (Luke 19:10 NASB).

Because of this gift, we can experience the forgiveness of sins. That is the great need of our lives. If I were to ask what are some of the great needs we have in our country, I would receive all kinds of answers.

"We need more relief programs for society's downtrodden."
"We need environmental protection."
"We need a formula for enduring peace."
"We need a guaranteed annual wage for all poor families."

"We need socialized medicine for the sick."
"We need greater political leaders."

But, friends, our greatest need is not something political, nor economical, nor educational. It is something spiritual. There is the problem of sin. Because of sin, our greatest need is salvation. We needed a Savior! On that holy night the answer came. God gave us His Son—*the world's greatest gift*. Luke 19:10 says He came "to seek and to save that which was lost."

Let us go to a fourth standard in determining the value of a gift.

IV. A gift may be determined valuable because of the *cost* involved.

A package may be large, heavy and ornately decorated. This does not indicate its value. You cannot judge a gift by the wrappings. External appearance can be deceiving.

What price was paid for that gift you received? How expensive was that gift? A gift may be deemed valuable based on the cost to the giver. The coming of Jesus was our greatest gift because it involved the greatest cost. Examine what this gift cost.

A. It cost heaven its brightest jewel.

God the Father gave something very precious. Christ was the crown jewel of heaven.

B. It cost the Father His only Son.

God the Father gave His very best—that which was dearest to His heart. This was a gift of inestimable worth. He gave us His Son.

C. It cost Jesus His life.

What a tremendous cost—a cruel death on a cross. He who knew no sin became sin for us "that we might be made the righteousness of God in Him" (II

Corinthians 5:21). Christmas was costly.

Another Christmas season will soon be passed. We should be thankful for all the material gifts we receive from our loved ones. But we should not fail to be grateful for our greatest gift. By all standards, Jesus is the world's greatest gift.

He is a wonder that can never be exhausted.
His is a story that never can be fully told.
He is a marvel that never can be fathomed.
This is the world's greatest gift because of its motivation.
This is the world's greatest gift because of its purpose.
This is the world's greatest gift because of its uniqueness.
This is the world's greatest gift because of its cost.

> Who is He in yonder stall,
> At whose feet the shepherds fall?
> Who is He in deep distress,
> Fasting in the wilderness?
> Who is He the people bless
> For His words of gentleness?
> Who is He to whom they bring
> All the sick and sorrowing?
> Who is He who from the grave
> Comes to succor, help, and save?
> 'Tis the Lord! oh wondrous story!
> 'Tis the Lord! the King of glory!
> At His feet we humbly fall,
> Crown Him! crown Him, Lord of all!
> —Benjamin Hanby

"Thanks be unto God for his unspeakable gift" (II Corinthians 9:15).

Members of Schmul's Wesleyan Book Club buy these outstanding books at 40% off the retail price.

800-$S_7P_7B_2O_6O_6K_5S_7$

Visit us on the Internet at www.wesleyanbooks.com

Schmul Publishing Company | PO Box 776 | Nicholasville, KY 40340

www.ingramcontent.com/pod-product-compliance
Lightning Source LLC
LaVergne TN
LVHW051600070426
835507LV00021B/2690